HOW TO MANAGE REAL ESTATE

BY

Lisa Turner – Brandon Phillips

Disclaimer

All information contained in this book is given for informational and educational purposes only. The author is not in any way accountable for any results or outcomes that emanate from using this material. Constructive attempts have been made to provide information that is both accurate and effective, but the author is not bound for the accuracy or use/misuse of this information.

Foreword

First, I would like to thank you for taking the first step in trusting me and deciding to purchase/read this life-transforming eBook. Thanks for spending your time and resources on this material.

I can assure you of exact results if you diligently follow the exact blueprint I outline in this information manual. It has transformed lives, and I strongly believe it will equally transform your own life too.

All the information I present in this Do It Yourself piece is easy to digest and practice.

Contents

Introduction

Rental property investment is an amazing choice for investors.

If you're searching for rental property investment, then you need to be very cautious. Before you set on your journey for a rental property, make sure that you really understand what it takes to be a landowner. Even though it is a gainful endeavor, it's anything but a snap. You would need to keep up the property so as to receive the monetary benefits throughout the time of your ownership.

To many, rental property investment is basically something that includes purchasing a house, putting it on lease, and then rounding up the bucks while relaxing on a sofa. Nonetheless, this is a long way from being realistic, particularly, if you want normal rental income for a considerable length of time to come. Stowing a rental property and accumulating a sound rental income for a year or two is only a commonplace undertaking. In any case, keeping up an durable rental income until you sell the property is take a lot of effort on your part.

As an investor, there is nothing more awful than keeping an empty rental property. This is on the grounds that you would need assets for the upkeep of the property, which isn't giving you any profits as it's empty. Consequently, you ought to effectively look for tenants and do whatever is conceivable to keep them happy. This includes paying attention to their requirements and making convenient repairs. Even though you may do some paltry repairs without anyone else's input, other complex undertakings (fixing channel holes and windowpanes) are best left to a specialist.

As you continue to look for rental property investment, it is essential that you think about the area. This involves separating the property from your living arrangement, the accessibility of the tenants, the normal lease that you can gather, and the capacity of the tenants in the region to pay you. A few districts may be more helpful than others. For example, it is smarter to lease a house close by a school, since many people will want a home in the region of their school. This will result in a plentiful inventory of tenants throughout the entire year. In a substance, rental property investment is tied in with investigating the area, taking the necessary steps to lease your property, keeping your tenants happy, and maintaining the property so it tends to be leased for a long time year after year, thereby limiting the opportunity time frame.

Investment in rental property can be a dangerous recommendation if the investor has not done his/her homework. In any case, it tends to be rewarding for the investor who makes an effort to look into it. Presumably, the one thing most investors need to know more than everything else is how they can wind up wealthy in the briefest timeframe by putting resources into rental property.

Most investors are focusing on flipping single-family houses when they ought to focus on putting resources into multi-nuclear families. With a solitary family house, if you lose the leaseholder, you have lost 100% of your income, which could be your benefit for a whole year. If you have a four-family condo and lose a tenant, you have three different families giving you checks to pay your costs. The primary concern is income, and income is more prominent with multi-nuclear families than with single-nuclear families.

If you have put resources into a few single-family rental properties, then you will more than likely need to make a trip to a few distinct areas to gather installments, or to mind the property. With one multi-nuclear family, you spare time, gas and mileage on your auto by just going to one area to gather a few installments, or to keep an eye on

3

your property. With the present economy, it could cost from $2,000-$7,500, depending on where it is located in the nation and the size of the house. Increase that by six, and you're talking a huge measure of cash. Fixing a six-family home would cost between $5,000-$10,000. You can figure it out.

There are a plenty of real estate masters with infomercials talking about the cash to be produced by flipping houses. They make I tseem simple. Before long, you will see that rehabbing a house tends to be exorbitant, particularly if you don't check the house in great detail a long time before purchasing. Costly, yet very tedious. Also, there are various short-term workers you need to manage. That is another issue; setting aside the effort to meet and research every one of those temporary workers. All things considered, you need somebody who knows what they are doing, isn't that right? When you locate a decent temporary worker, and he has done work for you, don't figure they will consistently be prepared to jump when you call them. All things considered, they are specialists, and they can't lounge around waiting for your calls. They have different jobs like all great representatives.

Don't misunderstand me; investment in rental property is a decent business. Single-family houses are wise investments. Yet, they can also be a way of putting resources into condos. If you know any individual who is making cash flipping houses, the chances are great that the person additionally has a few condos in their portfolio. Flipping houses is fine for the individual who needs to do it; however, investment in rental property is a better investment. Furthermore, there is an enormous market for condo contributing. Investment in rental property is a sound business.

The central objectives of any property investment are gratefulness, income and expense reserve funds. Rental property investment is the main property investment that gives you all of these three advantages simultaneously.

CHAPTER ONE
Why ou Should Invest in Real Estate

Have you ever wondered, "Why put resources into land?" The appropriate response may rely on numerous things. You may search for capital gratefulness, a regular month to month income, improve your expectations for everyday comforts to help different people who need better lodging. You may also need a home to live in and raise a family. While capital development is a principle explanation behind a great part of the contributing that is finished by people and organizations, there are different reasons that you can exploit.

You may not understand that acquiring a home in which you live can be incredible speculation. The correct cost on a home means that you can have a long haul interest in your place of living arrangement. Picking the correct area and consulting to get the correct cost is significant when you are looking for a venture to develop. The best way to purchase a home that increases in value is a sort of authorized investment fund plan.

There might be speculation choices made that upgrade the expectation for everyday comforts for the speculator. A superior neighborhood, where to live or a better home, will be an expansion in the estimation of the property claimed. The way of life can also be expanded when there is more income, as in interest in business property. Flipping houses can also expand your way of life if the tasks are chosen carefully.

Another motivation to put resources into genuine property is that it can give positive income every month, as well as long-term appreciation. If you like the possibility of the pay, yet aren't sure about the issues that come with the tenants, you could employ a property board organization to do the communication with the tenants and screening. You procure some portion of the month to month rental or rent expenses and normally, the property increments in incentive simultaneously.

A few speculators may be associated with charitable associations or non-profit groups whose aim is to provide lodging accessible to the individuals who can't afford the cost of lodging. Helpful issues are not as regular as reasons for property speculations, yet it happens on occasion. This is a substantially more sorted out methodology and one that generally requires a collective effort. Something else you may not have considered about putting resources into land is that it is a means of broadening your portfolio.

Broadening your portfolio will provide assurance against any misfortunes that could happen when you have just one kind of speculation vehicle. Land speculations complete the components expected to have a balanced group of venture decisions.

Another explanation behind putting resources into land is the financial specialist appreciates the inventive procedure of getting a property and returning it to valuable condition. The property may be improved enough for it to be leased, rented or exchanged. The reason might be due to a solid structure or reconstructing a property that generally would keep on falling apart. This kind of speculation is a delightful innovative encounter for certain individuals. It benefits the area and the individuals who have an incredible spot to live.

If you see answers to the question, "Why put resources into land?" in the abovementioned, you are well on your way to achieving an increase in your capital speculation. You can construct a portfolio that shows great returns without being unsafe. Land is an astounding decision and has a decent number of chances. You shouldn't have to spend a lot of cash if you pick your ventures cautiously.

Putting resources into land will consistently be a tremendous chance, and your progress relies upon the systems you use in the venture. Don't permit media promotion to stop you from taking part in the speculation opportunity. Your fantasy about getting to be effective in the business ought to be a drive.

Individuals will consistently require a sanctuary to feel safe, and if you can provide one, they will pay you for a long time, families need a home, and as a rule, they want an ordinary home that fits their financial limit and will happily pay their month to month rental. The intensity of having rentals is that as long as you have tenants, you will have a check each month. This is continuing income with no stress to the monetary exhibition.

In a circumstance where the bank's financing costs have diminished and the stores are yielding negligible returns, the securities exchanges are unstable and value is high-risk profile with lower returns. Conversely, property has consistently provided returns as far as riches go. Putting resources into the correct property gives you the chance to double your interest in a couple of years.

Almost certainly, your purchased properties will increase in value each year, and considerable income is a reality in the wake of deducting the cost of support and different charges like expenses, which are payable to the Government.

One territory that you should not neglect is the reality that you need a roused dealer. You should discover somebody who needs to sell right away. Ordinarily, they are in a difficult situation, close to liquidation, have a death in the family, are getting a separation or any number of different reasons.

Purchasing land for venture openings isn't inflated, yet it requires chance and having the option to conform to regularly evolving conditions. In doing so, you can build yourself a fortune after some time and snicker at all the media that told you not to go into land contributing.

Perhaps the best speculation you can make is to purchase procuring land. Particularly since the land market has crumbled in numerous territories in the nation, you can purchase property at much lower costs than what they were going for a couple of years back. Over the years, the value increment of the property alone will give you a pleasant benefit, equivalent to that of numerous stocks. However, there are different focal points.

When you purchase stocks or bonds, you put them in a safe or at your bank, and that is it. You can't do anything with them. Land then again gives you something you can use and produce income with (you can live in it yourself or lease it out).

Regardless of how you turn it, land is a rare opportunity; there is no (simple and modest) approach to make more land than there is now, regardless of what they say in Dubai. With a developing populace, the estimation of land can rise, particularly in thickly populated regions. So, if you purchase land now, you have nearly ensured a decent benefit as long as you hang onto it long enough.

Zoning sheets decide how certain zones of land can be used: horticulture, private, industry... In many networks, these zoning sheets have a traditionalist position that stays away from quick development since that also comes with its very own issues and costs. So the accessible land that can be used for private living won't be extended rapidly, implying that the estimation of the available properties will go up.

If you are somewhat of a jack of all trades, you can redesign land property inexpensively by doing a great deal of work, or you can re-appropriate it. Frequently, little costs go far to expanding the estimation of the property significantly. There is a whole industry of property engineers that purchase property well underneath its potential value, and by making the correct redesigns, you can make a clean benefit in a brief timeframe. It also requires some investment, experience and a spending limit to find genuine jewels.

Another enormous bit of leeway of land is that you can obtain a ton of cash to get it, up to 80-90% of its complete value. This is called influence, and with just a little venture of 10 to 20 percent, you can acquire something a lot more noteworthy. When the estimation of the property goes up, you profit on your venture and the cash you acquired.

If you choose to move into the house you got yourself; you can even deduct the tax you pay on your credit from your duties to truly add to the arrangement.

Try not to purchase land without intensive research and realize that you will lose more cash than you make in the initial couple of years when you are leasing the property to get it up to standard. Land should never be viewed as momentary speculation (unless you are an accomplished property designer who does transient purchase remodeling and selling activities).

There are six reasons why you should consider wholesaling land, particularly if you are new to land contributing.

In the first place, there is almost no money required to discount land. While you can start your wholesaling land vocation with positively no cash, it helps to have a minimal expenditure to use as real cash (under $100 as a rule) and some cash for advertising to help find interested vendors. Would you be able to begin wholesaling with a promissory note and do no cost promoting? Yes. Is it harder to do that? Yes. At any rate, you'd look at it; however, you won't require a huge number of dollars for upfront installments or holding costs for home loans while wholesaling.

Second, you can become familiar with your market and the business while you gain some cash. I wonder why a few people engage with rental land with almost no information of the business and particularly their market when you can, without much of a stretch, gain proficiency with the market and the business by investigating bargains and wholesaling them to an accomplished financial specialist as they learn. With wholesaling, you can start to win cash and get familiar with the business and your neighborhood land showcase simultaneously.

Third, you can develop your fantasy colleagues and system ahead of time. Having key colleagues set up can effect progress and disappointment. If you attempted to hold back to locate an incredible land record or legal advisor when you truly required one, it could be past the point of no return. That is the reason wholesaling is incredible; you can fabricate your key dream colleagues and your system of experts that will help you in your business as you start wholesaling.

Fourth, you can build your purchasers list. It is insane to engage in land contributing and not assemble a purchasers list ahead of time. Why would you ever hold back looking for property and are making payments on it before beginning to search for purchasers? With wholesaling, you can build your purchasers list, make contacts with different financial specialists and deal tracker owner tenant purchasers while you are searching for discount properties.

Fifth, you can subside into your specialty. There are bunches of specialties in land contributing from single-family homes to multi-units, from private to business, from purchase and lease to fix and flip and heaps of varieties in the middle. Wholesaling enables you to perceive what different financial specialists are doing, gain proficiency with the advantages and disadvantages of different specialties, and choose what specialty you will focus on. You may discover you are drawn to just wholesaling.

Sixth, you can figure out how to create quick income with certainty. Depending on the specialty you center around, income difficulties will probably become an issue sooner or later. You need an approach to have the option to create snappy pieces of money to keep your speculations and business running. That is the place where wholesaling comes in for some financial specialists, and having wholesaled a lot of arrangements for huge compensation can facilitate the pressure of the income crunch.

All in all, the six reasons above are the reasons I firmly prescribe to everybody keen on land contributing to figure out how to discount property- particularly if you are just starting out.

Is it accurate to say that with the economy battling, this is the best time to contribute some of your additional cash in land. A great many people that got into land did as such in 2005-2007, and as you realize, the market crashed and has never recovered. You may be afraid that this might happen again, and that point is a substantial one;

however, presently, it's a good time to put resources into houses, as the market is going to take a jump very soon.

For a very long time, individuals consistently have imagined that the main land venture they required was their very own home; however, that time has changed. With regards to building your total assets and making a significant resource for retirement, the one thing that will consistently be there is your home. I realize that putting resources into land can be alarming, particularly when such huge numbers of individuals are selling; however, in all actuality, they are selling since they can't afford the cost of their home, and if you can afford it, then it is just a matter of going to a reasonable cost.

The reason why it's a good time to put resources into land is that when the market and everything else become horrific, many people will sell anything they have simply to endure, and if you can give them what they need in return for taking on their home at a low value, then why not do that? What I would prescribe doing is attempting to get a bargain deal. The lower the cost when you purchase the home methods, the better the land bargain in the end. Simply realize that tossing out a low offer is certifiably not an awful thing if the merchant acknowledges it, and at that point, it is just as much their choice as it was yours.

Another motivation is that the loan fees continue dropping. Something that you have to understand is that purchasing should go up when the loan fees go down, yet four years ago, that did not occur by plan. Help yourself out and put resources into homes; don't be sorry for not listening to my advice.

Make sure you understand that you need enough cash when putting resources into houses because the economy is set for another downturn, and it would not bode well to back a whole home.

A career in the land business can be extremely fulfilling, be that as it may, you have to continue on and make a solid effort to accomplish achievement. If you are profoundly energetic and driven, then becoming a realtor may be an ideal career for you. It is a profession that can give you satisfaction and achievement as long as you realize how to approach the market. Today, there are currently ever-increasing numbers of people who are moving their profession and becoming a specialist because of the possibility of extraordinary wealth and the straightforward manner of getting a permit. Recorded below are more reasons why you should consider turning into a land deals specialist.

Adaptability: One of the primary reasons why a career in the realty business is worthwhile is the adaptability with which you can carry on with your life. If you are considering working low maintenance specialist, you can, in any case, have different occupations which can fundamentally build your pay. This career also makes it feasible for you to invest energy with your family while acquiring commissions. Besides being more responsible for your time, you also don't need to manage a boss or executives. The primary manager you have is the dealer responsible for the realty organization you are working for.

Potential Growth in Business: With this career, there are no restrictions for development. All you need is to stay driven and have an appropriate hard-working attitude, and you will receive the benefits. Be that as it may, to accomplish achievement, you have to sharpen your business abilities and establish a compelling marketing methodology.

Also, the potential outcomes are huge. Even though the organization you will work for will take a specific rate from your bonus, the degree of income you will get is still fulfilling. Keep in mind that the measure of pay you get will depend to a great extent on the measure of time and effort you contribute. You can develop your business by using an associate, or you can get a representative permit to assemble a financier. Thus, you can support specialists to build your business.

Associations: If you have been living in similar territory for a long time, it is conceivable that you have made associations with different individuals, for example, individuals in your neighborhood, your companions, etc. An occupation in land is extremely lucrative if you already have an established customer base.

When you get into this profession, you should promptly tell your contacts that you can help them with their realty needs. If you have enough associations with ideal individuals, you won't need to get on the telephone and call others. You can simply depend on the suggestions of your customer base.

The fundamental explanation you ought to put resources into property is to make an exceptionally positive advance for verifying your future and that of your family. Land is conceivably the most used speculation device the world over, yet a great many people don't think of it as a venture. Even more surprising is that the vast majority are instinctually great at land; they are basically specialists now, but they simply come up short on some fundamental devices to get them on their way.

Owning your own house is regularly depicted as the dream of a family, yet that is constraining. You may think that once you have your own home, then you've arrived at the summit, and you ought to kick back and be glad of your achievement. When you've satisfied the bank loan on your property, you own the property, by and large. You may have even made some capital increase with an ongoing valuation. That is incredible; however, you can accomplish more.

The incredible thing about land is that there are numerous systems, venture styles, procedures, research and looking strategies that exist, and the adventure is diverse for every individual. The facts demonstrate that there's a lot of cash to be made in land (anybody remember Donald Trump and Trump Tower?). Yet land can be an instrument for individuals who simply need a touch of additional cash, security for their retirement, or some property to enable their children to get a decent start in their adult life. All you need to accomplish your objectives - and they are yours alone, so you're liable for your disappointments the same as your triumphs - is some information.

I've discovered that property venture is an extraordinary leveler of individuals. A mogul will have a similar feeling of accomplishment and pride in a settled arrangement as a first home purchaser, which brings me to another point - having the funding to begin, or not having it at all. Some capital is important to finance a straight acquisition of a house. Yet there are many different alternatives to verify the property you need and bring the arrangement that you long for to the real world. As it were, don't give an easily overlooked detail like cash to obstruct your property speculation business.

While private contributing strategies are outstanding to numerous property financial specialists, many still don't think why they should or how to put resources into business land. If you notice land speculation, to the vast majority, you will likely wind up in a discussion overwhelmed by unscripted television energized private land moves.

Indeed, as a whole, we think about flipping private properties and all the cash that was made until the air pocket bursts. We get it! In any case, private land is valued in examination deals, so what happens when these deals are dropping like a skydiver without a parachute and the number of offers is evaporating? You're left with a property that you can't "turn and consume" in a short measure of time and conceivably one you purchased excessively high.

If you keep running into a solidified credit showcase and have home purchasers, who can't get contracts, your house will stay there, consistently draining you as you rack up conveying costs. While purchasing and selling or leasing houses has its advantages as a venture action, figuring out how to put resources into business land won't just help you possibly get more cash-flow; it will also widen your speculation horizons and give you some decent variety.

Business land comes in numerous structures and is basically any property that is possessed with the sole reason for making income for the owners. While single-family private homes do actually possess all the necessary qualities, they are not usually viewed as business speculations. Places of business, high rises, land, lodgings and different sorts of property are what we are looking at here when we are seeking how to put resources into business structures - lofts, malls, office space, and strip shopping centers.

Business land has a favorable position over private land in that its worth does not depend on correlation deals. Just because a place of business down the road went for $1 million doesn't mean yours will as well. When you put resources into business property, you do so dependent on the income it makes. Along these lines, if you need to build the estimation of your property, you basically figure out how to expand the income. This should be possible by expanding incomes like rents, stockpiling charges, distributing, or clothing or diminishing costs like upkeep or home loans.Business structures with an exceptional arrangement of difficulties and advantages.

Like some other ventures, you should gauge your risk resistance, cash, the time you have available for speculation, and what the commercial center is doing. Business land contributing is "easy street" that most low maintenance novices graduate to after they have fiddled with private land speculation. Financial specialists discover the capacity to control an incentive through expanding pay, broadening of risk through a large number and better influence as motivations to leave the private game to beginners and reality television stars.

CHAPTER TWO

Why You Should Want to Be a Landowner

What is a landowner?

A landowner is an individual or a business who possesses land and leases or rents the property for cash to another group. The leasing group is known as a tenant. Proprietors regularly provide the essential support or repairs during the rental timeframe, while the tenant is liable for the neatness and general upkeep of the property.

Separating Landowner

Landowners put resources into land as a source of money-related benefit. The financial advantages of being a landowner incorporate a constant flow of monthly tenant income, just like responsibility for inheritance property, which can possibly acknowledge in worth. Landowners have explicit rights and obligations, which vary from state to state, and there are general laws that are consistent with all states.

Owners reserve the right to collect rent, just like any prearranged late charges. They also reserve the option to raise the rent as characterized in the tenant-landowner rent understanding. When tenants don't pay the rent, owners reserve the option to remove them. The procedure of removal also changes from state to state. Most states furnish landowners with the capacity to collect leases just like legitimate expenses.

Landowners are liable for keeping up their investment properties in a reasonable condition, overseeing security stores, and guaranteeing that a property is spotless and empty when another tenant moves in. The landowner should also follow all nearby construction laws, carry out brief repairs, and keep every crucial help, including plumbing, power, and warmth, in working order.

A security deposit is additionally a basic commitment for any owner. While owners reserve the privilege to charge tenants a security deposit to cover both property damage, just like unpaid lease, the deposit never really has a place with the landowner. There are standards and laws administering security deposits and how they should be maintained. These standards shift from state to state. Landowners who breach these laws could confront legitimate consequences.

The Advantages and Disadvantages of Being a Landowner

Landowners have budgetary points of interest and inconveniences when putting resources into an investment property. Among the advantages, a landowner may use obtained assets to buy an investment property; in this way, requiring a smaller part of the complete property cost to pick up the rental payments from the structure. The investment property can verify this obligation, opening up different resources having a place with the landowner.

Moreover, most expenses related to investment properties are charge deductible. If there is no net benefit after costs, rental income is basically untaxed income. As the investment property home loan is squared away, landowners increase the ownership level of their property and access the valuation for its worth.

Be that as it may, when an owner sells a property, they will make good on government obligations on any capital increases unless they turn over the cash into another investment property. This procedure, called a 1031 trade, has explicit prerequisites. Any new property must be recognized inside 45-days of the deal, and the full move must happen inside 180 days.

A Tenant Disappears from a Rental Property - What Should a Landowner Do?

From multiple points of view, it's the landowner's worst possible nightmare.

As the owner, you turn up one morning out of the blue, and there it is; your purchase to-give property, a chance to empty and deserted like the 'Mary Celeste.' With any karma, the tenant has quite recently abandoned the property and their assets and none of your private speculation property. Shockingly, this happened to me one New Year when I arrived at my private venture property to find that half of my new kitchen had also been appropriated, along with another washing machine and refrigerator. To make things worse, as I was processing this data, I heard a knock on the door. It was a prospective tenant coming to view my purchase to-let property. I was entirely confused.

What to do?

The main thing a landowner shouldn't do is over-respond and alarm. Take a deep breath and try to avoid panicking.

Tragically, if there are no constrained indications of passage, at that point, purchase to-let substance protection won't cover a landowner for their misfortunes. A landowner should reveal any robbery to the police so that should you make up for lost time with your tenant, at some stage, the degree of your misfortunes are recorded and can be checked.

The other thing is, a landowner should not presume that the tenants have absconded and change the locks. A tenant's disappearance doesn't finish a tenure, even where the tenant never pays the lease again and has taken a large portion of the owner's kitchen, as in my specific case. What an owner needs to do is follow the law to finish an occupancy by either giving a segment 8 or segment 21 notice.

Landowners following a tenant

Firstly, an owner ought to guarantee that they acquired ownership of their purchase to-let property legitimately to empower them to re-let their private venture property. Proprietors will also need to guarantee any monies they get before the tenants vanished. This will presumably include prosecuting the tenant.

The issue with taking court procedures against a tenant is that an owner needs their location to serve them the authoritative reports.

The procedure for a landowner following a tenant can be simple or it might demonstrate to be inconceivable, especially where a tenant is a 'proficient tenant' and is experienced at doing a bunk and abandoning their obligations while vanishing into the 'ether.' The initial step an owner should use to follow a tenant is to gather a wide summary of data that a landowner has on the tenant. An owner should have some essential details because of the first credit check they carried out on the tenant. Data, for example, like past location and date of birth, will be valuable in having the option to conceivably follow the absconded tenant.

For example, an owner could then use these details and use an organization like, for example, Tracemart, to attempt to find the tenant.

On the other hand, a landowner could use a specialist investigator who can do all the leg work for the owner. First, find an investigator who will work on a no outcome, no expense premise. This administration will cost an owner $35. They also offer owners a follow and gather service, which implies that they will take the necessary steps to collect the obligation, just like following the tenant.

When an owner has a tenant's address, they are capable of making a legal move through the courts against the tenant to recover the obligation.

Landowners using a private investigator

Where a landowner has a huge obligation adding up to a few a large number of pounds and is sure that the tenant has a sizeable income or resources, then they could consider using a private agent. PI's aren't cheap, and you will look at paying $30+ every hour, which suggests that bills can certainly run into hundreds if not thousands of pounds. Be that as it may, a good PI might be able to get to data that you and I couldn't, and if that means finding an absent, expert tenant, it could be justified, despite all the trouble.

Expression of caution for owners

Nonetheless, here's an expression of caution additionally picked up from individual experience. Regardless of whether the landowner is effective in getting a County Court Judgment, if the tenant has next to zero income and no advantages, the sum that an owner will get could imply that a tenant will take numerous years to satisfy the obligation. The probability is that installments won't be nonstop. For this situation, an owner is correct in asking themselves whether it was worth the expense and effort, and this inquiry should be consistently asked right off the bat in any procedures.

Indeed, even where the tenant is working, and the owner gets a connection to a procuring order, the landowner will need the details of where the tenant is working. This is on the grounds that the owner or professional representing them will require the business' details so as to be able to keep in touch with them and teach them to make installments. The beneficial thing once this has been done is a connection of profit request, which implies that an owner's installment is automatically removed from their tenant's wages by a tenant's representative before they get their net wages, like tax is paid through PAYE (pay as you go).

Selling an owner's obligation

I have found out about certain owners who have endeavored to on-sell their tenant's obligation to a debt collection office. Actually, an owner who does this will renounce the greater part of their obligation. In any event, for example, an indebted person, who may also be a property holder, the most an owner is probably going to get from the debt collection organization is around 30 cents in the dollar or 30%. Where it's almost certain that this is an instance of a tenant that has slipped off and can't be followed; the sum an owner is probably going to get is in the low single figures - at the end of the day, viably nothing!

The significance of owners confirming their tenants

This features the significance of a landowner working more diligently in verifying the tenant.

This involves doing a credit check on their imminent tenant. Getting a decent tenant at the beginning will limit the odds that the tenant is probably going to flee. Where they do, a landowner should then have the basic data that will help to get some portion of their cash back should the tenant choose to vanish into the night!

What is a security deposit?

In its most straightforward structure, a security deposit is an entirety of cash given over by the tenant to an owner toward the beginning of rent as security for rent payments.

Security deposits for private premises are currently safeguarded by guidelines. A landowner must join a Tenancy Deposit Scheme, and the inability to consent to the guidelines qualifies the tenant to sue for pay equivalent to multiple times the valuation of the security deposit.

For business premises, there is no such security, in any case. Much of the time, landowners endeavor to use lease stores for an entire scope of purposes. If you are stressed over what your owner may do with the deposit once you have given it, then you need to guarantee that the landowner's privileges and commitments in regard to the security deposit are reported, either in the rent or a different security deposit deed. This is an essential initial step. If there is nothing recorded as a hard copy managing the security deposit, at that point, the landowner can place it straight into the bank and spend it.

Having established the principles concerning the use of the security deposit, it must then be recorded as a hard copy, and what things ought to be canvassed in the rent or security deposit deed?

• Who holds the deposit? In a perfect world, the landowner should not hold the deposit. In a perfect world, it should be held in a record managed by the landowner's specialist to guarantee that the assets are not misused. If the landowner goes into liquidation or is announced bankrupt, suing for the deposit will be an exercise in futility if the cash has been spent. It very well may be hard to convince an owner to consent to this (normally because specialists have no enthusiasm for dealing with the many deposits representing their customers). At any rate, if the owner is to hold the deposit, it ought to be paid into a different assigned security account.

• Who is qualified for enthusiasm on the deposit? This ought to consistently be the tenant as it is the tenant's cash. The rent or security deposit deed should determine that the owner place the cash into an account that pays premium interest and that the premium ought to be paid to the tenant (for the most part once at regular intervals). The interest should not simply be permitted to sit in the security account.

• Under what conditions can the landowner pull back cash from the security account? This should be thoroughly indicated. The proprietor's specialists will typically draft the documentation to enable the landowner to deduct cash whenever the tenant breaks the rent to cover all problems and costs caused by the landowner due to the break. Like reimbursements, this gives the landowner a privilege to pay any costs that the general law may not generally permit and is accordingly naturally uncalled for. The owner should just be permitted to pull back cash for non-payment of rent (and potentially enthusiasm on the unpaid lease if the rent accommodates enthusiasm on late rental installments). The landowner should also not be qualified to pull back cash for non-installment of administration charges as the explanation behind the non-payment might be a disagreement about the measure of the administration charge.

• When should the deposit be reimbursed to the tenant? The guideline behind the security deposit is that a landowner is qualified to request a security deposit where a tenant can't show his capacity to pay the rent (by delivering records or references to exhibit its budgetary position). That being the situation, the tenant ought to be qualified to get his deposit back if, at some point during the term, he can display his money-related quality. A typical method for managing this in a rental agreement deed is to state that a tenant is qualified to get back his security deposit if he can deliver three years accounts, which demonstrate a net benefit of multiple times the yearly lease. The security deposit ought to also be returned to the tenant if he sells the rent and furthermore, toward the finish of the term. Moreover, the owner must not reserve the option to deduct any sums from the deposit toward the finish of the term if it decides to cover a potential decrepitudes guarantee.

The owner-tenant understanding ought to be marked by both groups. It illuminates the obligations of each group when going into an agreement for a tenant to lease a house or condo from an owner. The landowner might be spoken to by a property executive organization.

Time is a key factor in tenant landowner understandings. If the understanding determines that it will be for a fixed arrangement of time, it is referred to as rent. Commonly, the two groups consent to a six-month or one-year term. If around then, the tenant wishes to broaden the rent, the individual may do as such by marking another rent with the owner.

Should the tenant not wish to be bound by another rent and the owner doesn't necessitate that another rent is marked, the tenant may remain in the property on a month-to-month period if the property owner acknowledges a monthly lease.

When considering a month to month rental, one must recall that it might be ended by either party, typically with 30-days notice depending on the state laws. In Nevada, if the tenant has been in the property for over one year and the landowner wishes to pull out to clear, the proposed time span to give notice is 60 days.

Rent and rental time spans are chosen in advance before the tenant moves into the property. Around then, a rental value, deposit terms and different conditions are arranged and set in motion for the two parties to sign. It is never a smart thought to do a verbal understanding. There are such a large number of issues that can emerge to cause problems for both the landowner and the tenant.

There are government codes that detail precisely what an owner needs to give in an investment property. Every territory may have marginally various laws. Yet all in all, the landowner needs to guarantee that when a tenant moves into the loft or house, it is sheltered and in a sensible, reasonable condition. There are specific necessities in administering the base norms for such things as plumbing and power, lighting, ventilation and without lead paint. The structure must have appropriate auxiliary trustworthiness. In certain urban areas, the owner should also provide a fire extinguisher and outfit the spot with a smoke alarm.

The owner not only needs to give a living space that is free of security risks, for example, uncovered wiring or broken sections of flooring, but is also answerable for keeping the tenants safe from wrongdoing. This implies outside entryways and available windows must have working locks. If there is a buzz-in radio, it must be utilitarian. Regular territories and stairwells must be sufficiently bright. The owner should also be certain that his/her tenants are not offenders and are not carrying out violations on the property.

The landowner is responsible for any repairs that must be made to the property during the leaseholders' occupancy. S/he should react to the tenant's requests for repairs inside 24 hours and have the repair completed inside a sensible time allotment. Tenants reserve the right to retain lease payments if repairs are not done, or to have the repairs done themselves, deducting the expense from the rent. If the circumstance isn't solved, they might have the option to sue or to break the agreement and leave in the rent timeframe. As a rule, landowners attempt to stay away from such measures by tracking when a repair request is made and when it is managed. What's more, they may take out risk protection (in certain states, this is required). Risk protection takes care of restorative or lawful costs that may emerge if the owner is sued for any damage endured by the tenant through carelessness, separation, security attack or improper eviction.

CHAPTER THREE
The Penalty of Landlording

Default of Rent

An owner should stay away from a protracted expulsion process — which can regularly take up to two months — or maintain a strategic distance from the risk that the tenant will pay the lease due when he gets the opportunity to court; however, will quit paying again directly after the court date. For reasons unknown, you can't just keep your tenant out of the home. Rather, you should go through legitimate lawful channels and prosecute him to get an eviction request first.

Issue Tenants

Some of the time, tenants cause issues at the investment property, for example, upsetting or harassing different tenants, directing criminal operations out of their home, or breaking different provisions of the lease. Once more, you should go through the lawful framework. You can't make unapproved moves individually.

Occupant Complaints

An owner may attempt to fight back against tenants who have submitted questions about the investment property. The tenant may have submitted these questions to the landowner or might have documented a proper objection with the region or state. In either case, you can't respond by raising the rent or documenting an eviction activity. You can't bug the tenant or make their living conditions so awkward that the tenant leaves the property, for example, by declining to make important repairs.

You Want to Charge More Rent

Sometimes, an owner needs out of the investment property, so he can charge more rent to another tenant than he's presently getting for the unit. This ordinarily occurs with rent balanced out condos or lofts where ensured tenants live.

The rent can be increased by a specific rate every year in rent-balanced out condos, so a tenant who has been there for a long time may pay far below market cost for the unit. Ensured tenants are comparable in that you can just increase the rent by a specific rate every year. These tenants can't be evicted for quite certain reasons.

You Don't Want to Rent to Certain Tenants

You can't stop certain tenants from leasing your property—this possibly falls into the region of separation. A landowner may want to keep her property for just adults, or she won't want people of a specific race or religion living there. She should abstain from making sensible lodging to the property for a tenant with a disbility.

Declining to lease for any of these reasons is illegal and can open you up to a genuine claim. A landowner is legitimately liable for adhering to reasonable lodging laws. There's a government Fair Housing Law, and most states have extra reasonable lodging decisions that landowners must follow.

An Increase in Property Expenses

A landowner may perform illegal activities to compensate for expansion in costs, for example, property charges, protection, utilities, or upkeep. This could incorporate attempting to get tenants to move who are paying lower rents, procuring unqualified tradespersons to perform repairs, or declining to schedule required property assessments.

Declining to Make Repairs

An owner is required to keep the investment property in a reasonable condition, so it's illegal to decline to make repairs that can influence a tenant's wellbeing or security. An owner may also make the repairs; however, unlawfully obtain unlicensed temporary workers to do the work, for example, electrical or plumbing that the town requires authorized experts to perform.

An owner may know about a wellbeing or security issue at the property and attempt to cover it up as opposed to fixing it. For instance, there could be a known lead paint danger. The landowner could attempt to stay away from expensive lead paint remediation by repainting over the danger rather than removing it. This is overstepping the law.

Entering the Property Without Proper Notice

Another disallowed demonstration isn't regarding a tenant's lawful right to protection. You reserve an option to enter a tenant's loft in a crisis; however, you should give the tenant appropriate notice in practically all different circumstances. The degree of notice is normally outlined in your state's owner/tenant laws and if not, it ought to be obviously expressed ahead of time in your rental agreement.

Notwithstanding appropriate notice, the owner can just enter the condo for lawful reasons, for example, to demonstrate the unit to prospective tenants or to make repairs. A few owners will put cameras or recording equipment inside a tenant's condo. This is totally unlawful, regardless of what the thinking is behind it.

Increasing the Rent

There are explicit guidelines for how regularly an owner can increase a tenant's lease and the amount she can build it. A landowner must give legitimate notice, for example, 30 to 60 days before a rent increase. She can't expand the lease by more than is lawfully permitted in her state, for example, by requesting a 10 percent increase when the greatest permitted by the state is 5 percent.

Not Getting Required Inspections

A few owners lease lofts without completing the necessary investigations first. A few states require another authentication of inhabitance or a livability assessment each time the unit is leased to another person, or now and again at regular intervals. A few states or towns require fire assessments before leasing, affirming that the unit has the best possible number of carbon monoxide or smoke alarms and that they're in working order.

Districts will regularly charge expenses for these examinations, which can run from several dollars to many dollars. Landowners should put off these reviews, so they don't need to pay these expenses. Try not to fall into this unlawful trap.

Making Illegal Deductions From the Security Deposit

A landowner may attempt to keep a tenant's security deposit for false repairs, damage to the property that really happened before the tenant moved in, or for other phony breaks in the rent understanding. Genuine motivations to keep a security deposit incorporate unpaid rent and harm to the unit, excluding customary mileage.

IT IS ILLEGAL FOR LANDLORDS TO HARASS THEIR TENANTS

Landowner harassment is illegal. California state law and nearby city mandates ensure tenants against harassment. Regardless of whether it's physical or verbal, all owner harassment has a similar objective—to drive the tenant to move out.

Harassment is the point at which a landowner uses diligent, forceful strategies, misrepresentation, pressure, or terrorizing to get a tenant to do what the owner needs. Harassment is intended to upset the tenant's legitimate right to feel pleasure in their home so as to compel the tenant to move out or to constrain the tenant from seeking any potential lawful rights they may have against the owner.

For what reason would an owner pester a tenant?

In lease controlled purviews, for example, San Francisco, Berkeley, Richmond, Mountain View, Alameda, and Oakland, owners are exceptionally motived to get long-term tenants to move out so as to raise the rent to market rate. Numerous owners depend on the fact that tenants don't have the foggiest idea about their legitimate rights. Harassing the tenant is sought after to keep away from expensive legitimate charges and the problem of a lawful eviction and, in particular, the owner ordinarily has no genuine reason to remove the tenant other than their dishonest desire to significantly raise the rent.

How can a tenant demonstrate harassment?

Owner harassment cases can, at times, be hard to demonstrate. These cases frequently boil down to a tenant's capacity to demonstrate the provocation. It is significant for tenants to be very tireless in recording each annoying occasion. Occupants ought to keep a log with dates and times. If conceivable, they should also get statements from friends and neighbors, and take pictures and chronicles. If a tenant feels that they are in physical threat, they should call the police and can also seek a restraining order against their owner.

What are the provocation laws in the State of California?

It is illegal for a landowner to prompt a tenant to leave a unit by using "power, tenacious dangers, or threatening behavior;" by taking steps to reveal the citizenship status of the tenant or the tenant's visitors; by entering the tenant's unit in considerable infringement of the law; and to take, deny, or expel the tenant's property from the unit without assent. Cal. Civ. Code § 1940.2.

Proprietors who are found to have bugged their tenants are subject to correctional fines of up to $2,000.00 for every infringement of the law. Id. Occupants don't need to be really expelled or productively evicted to be granted fines for harassment. Id.

Furthermore, the state's enemy of counter resolution keeps a landowner from bugging a tenant after the tenant has affirmed rights under the law. Cal. Civ. Code § 1942.5. Proprietors who abuse this preclusion are obligated for real fines, lawyer's charges, and correctional fines of up to $2,000 per retaliatory act. Id.

What are the harassment laws in the City of San Francisco?

The San Francisco Rent Ordinance shields tenants from landowner provocation. The mandate is broader than the California provocation resolution, and it incorporates a catch-all arrangement to cover whatever isn't unequivocally identified. S.F. Cal., Rent Ordinance § 37.10B. In San Francisco, landowners are explicitly denied from doing the following :

•   Interrupt, end, or neglect to give lodging administrations required by agreement or by state, area or neighborhood lodging, wellbeing or security laws; fail to perform repairs and upkeep required by agreement or by state, province or nearby lodging, wellbeing or wellbeing laws;

•   Fail to practice due diligence in finishing repairs and support once embraced or neglect to follow suitable industry fix, control or remediation conventions intended to limit presentation to commotion, dust, lead, paint, shape, asbestos, or other structure materials with conceivably unsafe wellbeing impacts;

- Abuse the owner's privilege of access into a rental lodging unit as that privilege is given by law;

- Influence or endeavor to impact a tenant to abandon a rental lodging unit through extortion, terrorizing or pressure;

- Attempt to force the tenant to clear with offer(s) of payments to empty that go with dangers or terrorizing;

- Threaten the tenant, by word or signal, with physical mismanager;

- Violate any law that forbids separation dependent on real or saw race, sex, sexual inclination, sexual direction, ethnic foundation, nationality, birthplace, migration or citizenship status, religion, age, parenthood, marriage, pregnancy, incapacity, AIDS or inhabitance by a minor youngster;

- Interfere with a tenant's entitlement to calm use and satisfaction in a rental lodging unit as that privilege is characterized by California law;

- Refuse to acknowledge or recognize receipt of a tenant's legitimate rent installment;

- Refuse a rent check for more than 30 days;

• Interfere with a tenant's entitlement to security;

• Request data that abuses a tenant's entitlement to protection, including yet not constrained to habitation or citizenship status or government managed savings number;

• Other rehashed acts or oversights of such importance as to considerably meddle with or upset the solace, rest, harmony or peace of any individual legitimately qualified to inhabit such unit and that reason, are probably going to cause, or are planned to cause any individual legally qualified for inhabitance of an abode unit to clear such abiding unit or to give up or postpone any rights in connection to such inhabitance. Id.

Occupants who are bothered by their owner can document a common claim against their landowner for harm and for an order to stop the conduct. Furthermore, an owner indicted for infringement of this area of the Rent Ordinance will be dependent upon criminal punishments. Id.

Where the tenant can demonstrate harassment, the landowner will be evaluated a statutory punishment of $1,000.00 for each occurrence of provocation. Id. The tenant can also look for an honor of multiple times (treble harms) their passionate trouble and out-of-pocket expenses. Id. Also, reformatory fines and lawyer expenses are accommodated under the law.

What are the harassment laws in the City of Oakland?

The Oakland Rent Ordinance's preclusion against landowner harassment is like San Francisco's mandate. Oakland, Cal., Mun. Code § 8.22.600. Under Oakland's Tenant Protection Ordinance (TPO), landowners will not do the following:

• Interrupt, end, or neglect to give lodging administrations required by agreement or by State, County or civil lodging, wellbeing or security laws, or take steps to do as such;

• Fail to perform repairs and upkeep required by agreement or by State, County or civil lodging, wellbeing or security laws, or take steps to do as such;

• Fail to practice due to steadiness in finishing repairs and support once attempted or neglect to pursue fitting industry fix, control or remediation conventions intended to limit introduction to clamor, dust, lead paint, shape, asbestos, or other structural materials with conceivably hurtful wellbeing impacts;

• Abuse the owner's privilege of access into a rental lodging unit as that privilege is given by law;

• Remove from the rental unit individual property, goods, or some other things without the earlier composed assent of the tenant;

• Influence or endeavor to impact to empty a rental unit through extortion, terrorizing or pressure, which will incorporate taking steps to report to U.S. Movement and Customs Enforcement, however that denial will not be understood as forestalling correspondence with U.S. Migration and Customs Enforcement with respect to a supposed infringement;

• Offer installments to the tenant to abandon more than once in six (6) months, after the tenant has advised the owner recorded as a hard copy that the tenant doesn't want to get further ideas of installments to clear;

• Attempt to pressure to clear with offer(s) of installments to empty that are accompanied by dangers or intimidation. This will exclude settlement offers made in accordance with some basic honesty and not accompanied by dangers or intimidation in pending eviction activities;

• Threaten the tenant, by word or signal, with physical damage;

• Substantially and directly meddle with the tenant's entitlement to calm use and pleasure in a rental lodging unit as that privilege is characterized by California law;

• Refuse to acknowledge or recognize receipt of the tenant's legitimate lease installment, aside from all things considered refusal might be allowed by state law after a notice to stop has been served on the Tenant and the timeframe for execution in accordance with the notice has terminated;

• Refuse to money a rent check for more than thirty (30) days, except if a composed receipt for installment has been given to the tenant;

• Interfere with the tenant's entitlement to security;

• Request data that abuses the tenant's entitlement to protection, including, however not constrained to home or citizenship status or government disability number, with the exception of as legally necessary or, on account of a standardized savings number, to get data for the capabilities for a tenure, or not discharge such data aside from as required or approved by law;

• Other rehashed acts or exclusions of such criticalness as to considerably meddle with or upset the solace, rest, harmony or calm of any individual legitimately qualified for inhabitance of such staying unit and that reason, are probably going to cause, or are expected to cause any individual legally qualified for inhabitance of an abode unit to empty such abiding unit or to give up or forgo any rights in connection to such inhabitance;

• Removing a lodging administration to make the tenant empty the Rental Unit. For instance, removing a parking spot, realizing that a tenant can't discover elective stopping and should move. Oakland, Cal., Mun. Code § 8.22.640.

Oakland's Tenant Protection Ordinance also precludes reprisal by the owner against the tenant for practicing their privileges under the law and enables tenants to bring counter cases against the landowner in common court. Id.

It is imperative to take note that under the Oakland TPO, tenants should initially agree to a notice necessity before they can seek after a common cure in court against their owner if the tenant claims infringement of 1, 2, 3, 10, 11, 12, or 13 recorded previously. Oakland, Cal., Mun. Code § 8.22.650. Occupants asserting an infringement of those subsections must advise the property owner or their specialist of the issue before recording a claim. Id. Also, on account of 1, 2, 3, 11, or 12 recorded over, the tenant must allow fifteen (15) days from the warning for the owner to address the issue. Id.

Like San Francisco's mandate, Oakland accommodates generous cash harms against landowners found subject for harassment. Oakland, Cal., Mun. Code § 8.22.670. Lawyer charges and costs, corrective harms, treble harms, and injunctive help are on the whole accessible under the statute. Id.

What are the harassment laws in the City of Berkeley?

The City of Berkeley additionally has a Tenant Protection Ordinance (TPO) that shields tenants from owner provocation and counter. Berkeley, Cal., Mun. Code § 13.79.060. The statute denies the landowner from doing any of the accompanying dishonestly:

• Influence, or endeavor to impact to abandon a rental unit through extortion or intimidation, or through unapproved physical acts;

• Threaten by utilization of misrepresentation, terrorizing, or pressure to end tenure, to recuperate ownership of a rental unit, or to evict a tenant from a rental unit. Such dangers will incorporate taking steps to report any tenant or visitor of any tenant to U.S. Movement and Customs Enforcement;

• Reduce, interfere, or retain any administrations or pleasantries gave to the tenant according to the tenant contract, custom, or law. Such administrations, however, are not restricted to arrangement of the tranquil use and pleasure in the rental unit;

• Interfere with any tenant's privileges of security. Unlawful obstruction with the tenant's entitlement to protection isn't restricted to mentioning data in regards to citizenship or residency status or government managed savings number of any tenant or individual from the tenant's family or family unit, tenant, or visitor of any tenant, aside from the motivation behind getting data for the capabilities for tenure preceding the initiation of an occupancy. Unlawful impedance with the privilege to protection additionally incorporates discharging any private data in regards to any individual depicted in this subdivision, aside from as legally necessary;

• Abuse the restricted right of access into a rental unit as built up and constrained by Civil Code 1954;

• Abuse, misuse, segregate, or exploit, any real or saw inability, quality or normal for any tenant, including, however not constrained to, the Tenant's cooperation in any segment 8, lodging decision voucher, or other sponsored lodging program;

• Fail to carry out any repairs in an auspicious and expert way that limits burden to the tenant; or neglect to practice due perseverance in finishing repairs and upkeep once attempted; or neglect to observe proper industry benchmarks to or conventions intended to limit presentation to clamor, dust, lead paint, asbestos, other structure materials with possibly destructive wellbeing impacts;

• Threaten not to perform repairs and upkeep required by agreement, custom, or law, or take steps to do as such;

• Fail to acknowledge or recognize receipt of the tenant's lease, or to immediately store the tenant's rent installment, or to expeditiously give a receipt to upon solicitation, aside from all things considered refusal might be allowed by state law after a notice to stop has been served, and the timespan for execution as per the notice has terminated;

• Offer installments to the tenant to empty without giving composed notice to the tenant of their privileges under this Chapter, using the structure recommended by City staff; anyway, this will not forbid offers made in pending unlawful detainer activities;

• Engage any tenant in any type of human dealing as characterized by California Penal Code segment 236.1, as a state of that tenants proceeded with inhabitance of a Rental Unit. Id.

Like the Oakland TPO talked about before, before the tenant can get a case common court for infringement of specific subsections recorded over, the tenant should initially consent to the notice prerequisite to the property owner or the owner's specialist. Id.

Landowners found to have disregarded the TPO can be obligated for genuine fines, lawyer charges, treble harms, order, and honor of common punishments in the entirety of somewhere in the range of $1,000 and $10,000 for every infringement. Furthermore, the owner might be held at risk for an extra punishment of up to $5,000 for every infringement against any individual who is handicapped or old (age sixty-five or over). Id.

What are the cases and harms in a tenant's claim against their owner for provocation?

As examined above, contingent upon which locale the tenant dwells, tenants can recoup a bunch of fines in a claim against their owner for harassment. A portion of the fines incorporate real fines, treble fines, correctional fines, lawyer expenses and costs, common punishments that fluctuate in sum contingent upon the city, and in certain wards, extra grants for crippled or older tenants are accessible.

Beside the provocation guarantee, different cases may seek after against the owner that will yield extra cash harms are for rupture of agreement and contract of very delight, unjust or productive ousting, and deliberate punishment of passionate misery.

Break of Contract and Covenant of Quiet Enjoyment:

Implied in each private rent is an agreement of peaceful happiness, ensuring that tenants will have the option to calmly make the most of their homes. Cal. Civ. Code § 1927. Where a landowner has considerably meddled with the tenant's tranquil pleasure in a unit, the tenant can sue for back rent. Through the utilization of master appraisers, the court will decide whether, and by how much, the rental estimation of the property declined because of the provocation. In Guntert vs. City of Stockton, 55 Cal. Application. 3d 131 (1976), for instance, the court granted back rent, where the landowner gave a few subjective eviction notices. Where a tenant is under consistent danger of removal, gets unlawful eviction, is verbally or physically compromised by an owner, and isn't profiting by convenient and appropriate repairs, the tenant can record a break of agreement guarantee against the landowner.

Helpful Eviction: If a tenant is constrained out of a lease controlled home in view of owner provocation, the tenant can sue for the expense to supplant the lease controlled home. At any rate, one court has enabled the tenant to recoup twenty years' worth of expanded lease. Where an owner is spurred by a craving to get a lease controlled tenant out from under lease control, this lease differential might be trebled (for example, significantly increased).

Deliberate Infliction of Emotional Distress: In instances of especially ridiculous lead, a tenant may sue a landowner in tort for purposeful curse of passionate trouble.

In the San Francisco case Richardson vs. Pridmore, 217 P.2d 113, the tenant endured unsuccessful labor because of being purposefully and unfairly evicted. The owner broke into the tenant's loft while they were away for a couple of days, putting all their stuff in a storm cellar, and changed the locks before giving the spot to new tenants. The jury granted the offended parties $7,250 ($63,910 in 2009 dollars) as pay.

CHAPTER FOUR
Do You Have to Manage Your Properties?

Numerous property executive organizations are discharging their new versatile help, which enables you to do everything that you've constantly done on your PC on your cell phone! I realize many are trying to figure out why they would need to use their cell phone to deal with their properties? All things considered, there are various reasons why you ought to consider going portable with your property executive business.

Here are a couple of reasons why using versatile assistance might be a smart thought for you:

•Service Requests - Maintenance workers can enter demands legitimately into the cell phone while out in the field. A cell phone will enable them to get to all the data they need while in the field; maybe they neglected to print a work order out before leaving the workplace or another request came in while they were out of the workplace. Versatile access will spare trips back to the workplace and will enable the support specialist to remain in the field and thereby, boost profitability.

•Resident Information - Mobile access will enable you to quickly see present and past tenant data, including lease and contact data, without returning to the workplace.

•Unit Status - If you are traveling and get a telephone call about a property and can't get to a PC immediately, portable access will enable you to rapidly look up property data to check things, for example, is the unit prepared, when will it be prepared or which units are accessible?

•Applicants - Perhaps an owner is out to supper and gets a telephone call asking about a property? The landowner could include their essential contact data on the fly, and when they return to the workplace, they would have the option to complete the application they began on the cell phone.

So you see, mobile access isn't only an "extravagant" term to use; it can give numerous advantages to your property executive business. Here's another reason how mobile access can add to your main concern business numbers. For example, what happens if a request for help comes in through the tenant gateway of your administration programming, or you get an assistance call, and the support specialist is out in the field at another unit? The administration request can either be retrieved or seen by the head of support and after that assigned, or perhaps it's simply you, so you can see the request and call to plan a time to go there, depending on your activities.

When the administration worker is in the field, they will be able to get the appropriate devices to go to the site where they would then be able to take pictures and send them back to the main office. Even though the photos can't naturally be attached, they can be sent if using a customer's email (for example, Outlook Express, Gmail, Yahoo, and so on.). Here, we see the excellence of the cloud with regard to data sharing. You'll never need to go back to the workplace to get a sheet of paper that would show the issue of a request. Everything should be possible in the cloud or in a hurry since now all the data required is conveyed through the cell phone.

I trust you presently observe the power of opportunity regarding dealing with your property on your cell phone. Maybe you can identify a few reasons why you should take your business through the cloud or recreate some of the ideas in this book for your own product or activities.

If you're choosing property website programming, appoint a Property Manager. We additionally have versatile assistance accessible to every one of our customers. We support iPad/iPhone Safari, Windows Phone IE9Mobile, and Android Chrome/Firefox programs. It will be ideal to note that customers using Firefox on Android-based tablets will be given a choice to shift back and forth between the full site and the mobile site by using a connection on the login screen.

If you have put resources into prime property in Brisbane, yet find that dealing with the property on a full-time premise is brimming with issues, at that point, there is no compelling reason to fuss. Your property portfolio can be effectively done with the mastery and capable direction of many counseling groups. While you have the alternative of experiencing traditional offices to deal with your property, as a rule, they flop pathetically to live up to your desires, as they don't have the bigger vision and are not presented to current venture components.

The staff at counseling organizations oversee properties of their own and accordingly have a more profound understanding of the way present-day land markets work. It is frequently observed that conventional offices rarely make a big deal about getting you the best rental costs for your excellent properties, and they regularly display a moderate methodology. With their forceful promoting systems and certainty coming from having multifaceted information about the rental evaluating and techniques in and around Brisbane, counseling organizations can enable you to get the best rental costs for your properties.

A first-rate dynamic and result situated methodology encourages them to get you the best protection assurance for your property. They can also get you quality tenants who are happy to pay the best rental costs that your property luxuriously merits. They know the futility of keeping your prime property empty for an extensive stretch – the longer the opening, the more significant the support cost and misfortunes due to loss of lease for the period. Counseling groups encourage you to deal with your property better than others by guaranteeing that the tenants are consistently kept happy and fulfilled by tending to their worries and settling their tenure issues in the quickest conceivable time.

They also guarantee legitimate association of all your property-related outgoings; for example, strata charges, group rates and water rates alongside the obligatory assessments. As a piece of better property, the executive administrations, they also make accessible at short notice, specialists and confide in individuals of different exchanges, for example, circuit testers, handymen and contractual workers, who can be trusted to give brief and exact administration at reasonable rates. Your property is assessed all the time, dependent on criticism from tenants and the fundamental course remedies prescribed to expand the intrigue and estimation of the property. This guarantees that your property is sought after by leaseholders, and you get the best rental rates with the goal that your venture potential is boosted.

Putting resources into land has been commonly considered as one of the great approaches to build your riches in the long-term. You may have purchased various properties as a result of specific reasons.

You may purchase a house to occupy yourself, or you may purchase a property for resale with the goal of picking up benefits from the transfer. Whatever the reasons, overseeing properties has progressed toward becoming a vital part of putting resources into land.

Anyway, what is the ideal approach to deal with your homes, condos or townhouses? One of the arrangements is to employ a property manager to deal with your land for your benefit. However, do remember the following focuses when employing somebody to oversee land for you.

Request reference

It may be valuable to request a reference from the property manager that you're thinking of employing. Talk to their current clients and check whether there are any complaints about them, particularly their capacity to manage land.

By and large, a great property manager ought to guarantee that your property is consistently leased, and ensure that the rent is dispatched to you in a suitable way. Aside from gathering the rent, they need to guarantee that your property is appropriately maintained and certified.

Paper Qualifications

Make sure you connect with somebody who has the important capabilities. Even though a paper capability isn't generally basic in guaranteeing that the property manager will work superbly; it helps you to survey their ability to take care of your properties.

If they are appropriately confirmed and approved, they will likely have the option to deal with your properties without you agonizing over the issues, for example, getting tenants for your properties, checking the background of the potential tenants, etc.

Most property owners realize how much duty is engaged with overseeing property, regardless of whether it's individual houses, units, condos or apartment suites. It requires some investment and effort, also cash. The owner of speculation property infrequently gets the opportunity to spend a week or even a day, at times, without a maintenance or tenant issue springing up.

There are some fine, dependable organizations to do this work for you. They're called property management services, and they can do quite a bit of your activity, however you see fit. If you don't like dealing with rent collecting and late installments, a property board administration can carry out that responsibility for you.

Truth be told, numerous venture property owners let a property management service handle everything to do with their rental or rent properties, and once in a while, they set foot on the premises!

What Does a Property Management Service Do?

Anything you need! A decent service has a group of gifted, reliable and secure workers that can deal with your properties so that the charge you pay the organization will really be worthwhile. When a tenant moves out, they will set up the unit for the next tenants and furthermore, promote the opening.

A property management service can deal with inside and outside support and finishing, employ outside contractual workers for significant repairs or redesigning occupations, keep your books, qualify planned tenants, handle removals, make good on your government obligations, and send you a monetary report as frequently as you wish.

They can also deal with obligation gathering, promote your empty units, and even handle advertising efforts. There is next to no property that the organization can't do with regard to expanding your income and keeping your units full.

Budgetary Cost Versus Genuine Cost

Some property management services charge a percentage of the rent, while others have a set rate scale. You might not have any desire to burn through cash to contract an administration firm; however, think about the option. When you use an authorized and reinforced property service, you'll have the option to carry on with your life with complete genuine feelings of serenity. There will be no more calls in the night for crises, no more stress over rents, and no more doing maintenance without anyone's help.

The expense of an administration is little when contrasted with the time and effort they spare you. You can even get assessment administration and finance incorporated into your administration understanding alongside stock control and bookkeeping administrations that incorporate yearly spending arrangement.

Picking the Right Service for Your Properties

If you choose to connect with property service management, look at their relationship as well as their notorieties. If they have a place with the AMO (Accredited Management Organization) or IREM (Institute of Real Estate Management), you'll realize that you're managing a firm that is regarded for their business ethics just like their fruitful administration.

Think about valuing and administration between multiple administrations, as costs can shift radically. It's a smart idea to choose what obligations you'd like to deal with yourself, assuming any, before you start dealings. You'll have the option to get the best charge and administration plan if that you have a firm idea of exactly what you need.

I've explained about the significance of taking the time in advance to prescreen your property manager to find one who has great finishing abilities. They must have sufficient education; obviously, that's essential. However, I stress that you truly attempt to discover how they maintain their business. Why? Once you hire them, you truly don't want to supervise them.

Partially, you will be "dealing with" your property supervisor, yet this movement ought to be restricted to the following:

To start with, when you've recently enlisted another property manager, your new property manager will require more consideration from you to ensure that the individual is the ideal individual for the activity, and that they are taking care of business right. Presently, "at the outset" can be a touch of misdirecting, because things may begin fine and go easily for a long time; however, the genuine test may not come until the first non-installment or eviction comes up. When it's time for the property manager to implement the rent, you may then realize that they are reasonable, yet firm. Your property manager should not be postponing removals since they accept the tenant's guarantee that they will pay in seven days, and so on.

Second, you will have intermittent chances to check in with your property manager when certain things come up. For instance, if you get a notice from the city about an infringement on your property, you have to refresh your property manager about it with the goal that they can deal with it. This is also a decent opportunity to check in and perceive how things are going. You can approach them about rental increments for upcoming lease renewals, inquiries concerning ongoing proclamations, request on maintenance to be done/that has been done, or about specific tenants who've been an issue previously.

You shouldn't have to advise your property manager to begin the removal procedure for somebody who isn't paying rent. They should be on it already! You shouldn't need to ask your property manager what is new with your properties - they ought to send you convenient communication on the majority of your properties and send you standard reports on any non-paying tenant using email, phone, fax or mail (in regard to where they are in the removal procedure or if they are on an installment plan, and so forth). Ultimately, your property manager should be consistently accessible to get back to you inside a sensible measure of time. There is nothing more disappointing than chasing down the individual who works for you!

If you have property to lease, you have to keep it maintained, which is a difficult activity to do, particularly if you are remaining ceaselessly. You can use landowner administration, which will do everything from fixing holes to giving complete support.

Leasing a property is an intricate assignment. It requires itemizing, from the appraisal of the property to ensuring that plausible tenants know about the opening. Frequently, the landowners remain far away from their property to be leased. Along these lines, they can't monitor every one of the details. In such cases, they can use property executive administrations to deal with everything in regard to the support and advertising of their property. For example, if you claim property in

Bromley, London, that you need to lease, you can contact capable nearby owner administrations.

Preparing the Property

To get tenants, your property needs to seem perfect, splendid, and fit for use. You can employ the landowner benefits that set up the property for your plausible tenants. As a matter of first importance, the specialists make an exhaustive appraisal of the property. Whatever work, cleaning, fixing or development is required in the property, they enlighten the owners and give free statements dependent on the examination. If you enlist them, they will prepare your property for your likely tenants. From minor repairs and rebuilding to make the whole property shining clean, they will work to your greatest advantage for organizing your property to draw in the tenants.

Unique cases - Free Your Time

Regardless of whether you have to fix broken showers, fitting entryways and bolts or get the property cleaned, you can call these services for unique cases. The erratic services given by support organizations incorporate just one-time maintenance of the property. Finding handymen, woodworkers, painters and electricity repair people to carry out the repairs appears to be a simple assignment; however, that isn't the situation. Furthermore, wouldn't it be good to get every single tradesperson at a similar spot? Employing a service will spare you time and help you cut back the costs too. While contracting these services, you should determine the things that should have been kept up alongside the way in which you need the experts to deal with these obligations.

Contracted Services - Free Yourselves

Using landowner benefits on agreement premise is significantly gainful for the individuals who live a long way from their properties. It is impractical for them to keep up these themselves. You can also liberate yourself from the obligations of dealing with your property if you live in another town and face problems. You can sign an agreement for the interior and exterior of the property. A few organizations even deal with the finishing. Each property needs inner support now and again, and contracting maintenance services will keep the weight off you. These agreements are either monthly or yearly. Unlike unique cases, you don't need to explain what should be done each time as the agreements are comprehensive.

Agreeable and Professional Services

Such services oversee property in light of a legitimate concern for the owners and mediate between the landowners and their tenants. When you search for property maintenance administrations, you should worry about certain things. Besides the territory the administrations gave, you should offer unmistakable quality to a few vital attributes. If you need development work to be done, you have to guarantee that the organization is acknowledged under exchanging models for structure contractual workers. Some things that should be considered are outlined below:

* Full assurance alongside protection.

* Ability to begin and complete the activity inside the stipulated time period.

* Electricians must be certified.

* They must have enlisted gas engineers.

* They should work with a lot of deliberation and consumer loyalty.

* Make sure they offer full quotations with no concealed expenses.

Finding a viable property, property management is anything but an overwhelming undertaking. Regardless of whether you dubiously search the Internet for landowner management, Bromley will go over various organizations in the area. In your selection, keep a record of the services you require and to check whether the organization is licensed or not.

A venture property can be a brilliant method to cushion your retirement fund, yet if that speculation property isn't in the state where you live, it also implies that you should deal with that property long separation. Similarly, like other long separation relationships, dealing with a property separation is something that requires incredible artfulness to draw off. It very well may be done, yet the difficulties can and do continue.

To ensure that you will have the option to deal with your property long separation, you must be certain that you are getting the correct tenants. This will obviously expect you to promote that the properties inside the region are available, yet the work doesn't stop there.

Before a tenant consents to lease or rent from you, they will certainly need to see the property. If you can't be there for that, then you need to organize for somebody to be there. When you have agreed with the planned tenant on a lease value, then you should do the following:

• Background Check: Running a record verification on every single prospective customer will tell you whether they've had any run-ins with the law that may perhaps discourage you from leasing from them.

• Credit Check: Another discretionary advance to take before leasing to anybody is a credit check. While it won't inform you about their character, it will reveal if they are 'late payers' or have done other crimes. Once more, this is something that may empower or discourage you from leasing to a forthcoming tenant.

• References: Always request references from the forthcoming tenants with respect to past owners. Ensure you get at least three and make an effort to call and talk with everyone. This is the most effortless approach to guarantee that you will be managing a respectable tenant.

When you have the correct tenant set up, it becomes an issue of correspondence. Great correspondence needs to come from the principle on your part too. An inability to convey information appropriately can be shocking.

Be certain that your rent or tenant contract explains in great detail what your obligations are and what the tenant's duties are; for example, grass care and general maintenance. Choose what you will pay for and give it a monetary value. For instance, say that you will pay any repairs that are over $40, and the tenant will be liable for smaller repairs under $40. This will shield the tenant from calling you ten times each day over each seemingly insignificant detail that turns out badly.

If the majority of this seems like it's a lot for you, then dealing with your property long separation may not be a good idea. You can generally procure a property manager that will deal with the majority of the regular occasions that accompany owning a property. Yes, they will cost you cash, yet this might be justified, considering all the trouble to you to guarantee that your long separation association with your precept remains as agreeable and prosperous as could reasonably be expected.

Have you purchased an Investment Property? Congrats. So,what do you do first? Try not to stress; you will do fine with some direction.

There are numerous masters who guarantee to tell you the best way to purchase or assume control over the property with no cash or credit. Some can!

Others demonstrate to you the conventional approaches to purchase land and make cash by leasing it. Nobody, however, shows you the most significant part of owning rental land, which is how to deal with your property without losing your shirt.

However, you gain investment property; the main issue that you need to manage is finding tenants. How would you get tenants who will assist you with making the repayments on this property?

All things considered, perhaps you do everything that you have to do. You get your first tenant. Is that all that you need? Is it happy ever after for the owner and tenant now? Try not to wager on it.

As you probably are aware, tenants are the soul of any investment property. Perhaps I should state great tenants. If you don't get great tenants, you can get so baffled that your wise venture will sharp on you, and you will search for somebody to buy the property, even at a loss.

There are temporary tenants. Plain and basic! Temporary tenants don't remain in one rental unit for long. They move around. The likelihood of you getting at least one of them is very high. In 20 years of overseeing rental land, I have seen unusual circumstances, including a tenant who nearly took several dollars from me. He is still out there, and thousands like him! Awful as that sounds, he was not my worst tenant.

There are a couple of procedures that new and prepared owners can set up to guarantee a fruitful relationship.

One must understand that this is a venture. You need your venture to develop and turn out to be progressively beneficial as the years pass by. You are currently placing a stranger in your property.

One of the main things that any owner ought to do when leasing their venture property is to have an agreement. There are "standard" contracts. You can use this as a format, yet include everything that you can think of. This will assist the planned tenant to realize that you value your property. You need them to dwell in it and appreciate it, yet you don't need them to "abuse" your property. "Abuse" of your property will cause its value to decline as opposed to up. I am certain that you didn't make a solid effort to buy a venture and then intend to reduce its value.

Leasing your empty property is an excellent recommendation. You are certain that there is the tenant to take care of your property and simultaneously, you acquire cash. With the present falling pattern in the market, leasing property is a protected method to win cash. However, looking for a decent tenant and keeping up your property isn't as simple as it might sound. Subsequently, you should hire property managers to do this work for you.

There are numerous organizations that do this work. All offer different management and charge in an unexpected way. It is important to experience the terms and conditions very well before going into an agreement with any organization. It is additionally great to compare their rates and different organizations offering these services.

Services they offer

There are different focal points in obtaining a property management organization. They are specialists in this specific field. They do the vital statistical surveying, lead the investigation of the property, and furthermore, do all the fundamental work to get a decent tenant. Without the assistance of these management organizations, it would be exceptionally hard to do the procedure on your own. It is tedious and exceptionally dull.

Therefore, it's better to hire one such organization and be free from all these issues.

The organization which you hire ought to have the option to release you from every one of the stresses of the legitimate angle. They must be able to assess your property and decide the most appropriate rent. Notwithstanding, if you feel that the lease expressed by them isn't right, then you can evaluate others. Other than deciding the lease for you, they additionally deal with all the legitimate issues which may emerge. They also help you to make choices on your money related to protecting your property, getting home loans and other comparable issues.

Extra help

Property managers are finished assistance given by these letting specialists. They publicize your property and get the best tenant for you. They generally attempt to welcome the estimation of your property, which thus builds your lease. These organizations weight the qualities of the house, which serve as a manual for the tenant.

Aside from every one of these services, property management organizations deal with all the authoritative issues of the property. The exchange of assessment bills to electric meter readings are dealt with by them. You are additionally certain to be guided by them to get suitable individuals for protection of the property. Subsequently, you can imagine that there are many duties attached to leasing the property. These are best considered by experts.

If you are new to taking care of your own property management, then the first couple of months will be a learning curve for you. There are various things that you will need to familiarize yourself with; however, one of the key variables to being effective at property is being composed. It is important that you do this from the beginning of your obligations. If you remember that property venture and property management is a business, then it will be a lot simpler for you to make the best possible condition. After all, you wouldn't maintain a complicated business and anticipate that it should be prosperous, so build up this equivalent mentality for your property management.

Perhaps the greatest obstacle to set up is your paperwork. Try not to be tricked into imagining that there won't be a pile of it because there will be. Here are a few types of paper classifications that you will be looked with and a few insights on the best way to keep them composed.

Ideally, you will have a PC that can assist you with the money-related parts of your property. However, this won't kill the printed paper copies that you'll need to deal with:

Tenant meetings, screening and rents:

It doesn't make a difference whether you are managing one tenant or fifty; you should still identify every tenant dealings exclusively. Hence, you have to have a tenant document. Along these lines, whenever you need data about a tenant, you just need to go to one source, which is that document. In this record, it is important to keep all the relevant data. The application structure, the pre-rental screening notes, receipts and rents. It's also a smart thought to keep a comment sheet that you can make a couple of notes if you need to give warnings or address other tenant concerns. These sorts of records are important if you ever need to make some kind of court move.

Requests:

If you own property, you can be certain that you will have loads of different costs. So, to truly follow your monetary data, you have to keep your

Requests classified. For instance, let's talk about repairs. There could be plumbing and heating or electrical repairs.

Keep separate documents for these Requests. Sure, you could simply stuff them across the board record; however, if you truly need to get the best out of your property venture, then you have to realize what is costing you cash.

For instance, lets say you have a different document for plumbing repairs. You start to see that this document is getting very full. At that point, it's telling you that you may have a genuine plumbing issue, and maybe you might need to make some increasingly significant repairs that will chop your costs down at last.

Receipts:

Normally, this will be a significant document, which demonstrates that you have received your month to month rental payments. There should be a record of the repayments on the tenants' documents; however, you also need a first-rate rental receipt document, where you can follow who and who has not paid.

As we suggested, your PC is going to help you with your record keeping. It is a good idea to have a printed copy of the data that is on your PC concerning your property management. If your PC crashes, then you are not stranded with regard to the day by day activity of what's occurring with your property.

Many individuals are into land speculation, yet they don't generally have the opportunity to go through a long stretch of time looking into properties and settling on a genuine choice about putting resources into a property. This is why individuals want to acquire the services of a property management organization to provide them with speculation experts, land specialists, temporary worker engineers, property consultants and land representatives. You may require the services and help of the previously mentioned land faculty as a rule; for instance, the choice of purchasing a home in a local area that is far from nearby markets or service stations. Another model is picking a structure for your business task or private venture that may harm your property and cause some genuine harm to nearby properties. As a non-land individual, you can't settle on these choices all alone. You need assistance, and this is where the property management organization comes in.

If you contract a venture expert to give you property management benefits, then you can be guaranteed that all your financing identified with the property will be taken care of productively and viably by them. The fundamental purpose for this is that these organizations have many experienced and educated consultants and property negotiators who know about each niche and corner of the place you are anticipating purchasing. They are the individuals who can enable you to make a superior choice before putting resources into a property for either business or private reasons. You can confide in them and take notice of their assertion when they state that a specific real estate parcel is advantageous while another isn't. These are the individuals who can prevent you from settling on an awful choice, which can make you lose your cash.

For instance, in the event of private undertakings, they ensure that all the mortgage holder charges and expenses are satisfied before you purchase the house. They go to all gatherings with you to ensure they have a full examination report about the amount you owe and what must be done to ensure you get the property you are keen on. They will deal with a wide range of installments between you and the vendor and ensure that the entire experience becomes simpler and more straightforward for you. Every one of your migraines and issues will turn into theirs.

A property portfolio is one device where you can get information, contacts, purchasers, and customers. A property portfolio is where you place all the important insights regarding your business. It will assist you in attracting more customers and persuade them that your property is great and beneficial for them.

As a property financial specialist, you should realize how to make a property portfolio. It is important for you since a portfolio is a controlling instrument to have prosperous speculation. To make a property portfolio, you initially have to claim property. Here are a few points on the best way to deal with a portfolio.

The first is doing your examination. You should set aside some effort to look into where the best investment properties are before developing a list of properties. You should discover properties that produce positive income. When we state income, it refers to the benefits you will achieve after your property repayments are deducted.

You should also decide on the lease interest. The best thing in speculation is that your tenant's investment property will take care of the entire expense of your home loan repayments. Be that as it may, if your property stays empty for quite a while, it is currently your obligation to cover the tab. So it is critical to realize the occupancy request before contributing to a property. Ensure that there is a short-hold tenancy understanding. It is essential when you are developing a tenancy agreement to verify every one of your privileges.

If you have a small property portfolio, you ought to have the option to acquire bargains through it. You may consolidate your portfolio with interests in various markets and areas. There are a few interesting points. You should ensure that you can support the task, even in the most pessimistic scenario. You may need to contribute to a property if the rental income doesn't take care of the expenses of protection and home loan repayments. Remember that continuous increments in the lease mean keeping your property in great condition.

You may improve your property portfolio by having the right choices and procedures in advertising, appropriate financing and enough planning of cash, and obviously, there ought to be correct sources. If you are set up with all these, your property will certainly increment simply like what you need.

CHAPTER FIVE

The Laws for a Landlord

With being a landowner comes numerous obligations. If you are a landowner, it is your obligation to guarantee the security of your tenants, and there are legitimate rules that must be adhered to.

A landowner will have an agreement with their tenants. As a rule, this will comprise archives marked by all gatherings. It is lawfully official, so the terms inside it should be deliberately considered. There are specific details that must be incorporated by law, and different things can be incorporated at the landowner's discretion. This can incorporate certain guidelines regarding what must be done and what is impossible by the tenants. For instance, a landowner may state that their tenants are not permitted to smoke in the home. Whichever landowner obligations are outlined in the tenure agreement must be adhered to, else you are breaking the agreement with your tenants.

It is the owner's responsibility to ensure that every single essential repair is made. This isn't the duty of the tenants. For instance, any basic repairs must be finished just as different repairs to things, for example, plumbing. Albeit tenants must take care of the home with due consideration, normal damage can occur, and this is the obligation of the owner.

Practically all owners require a deposit before tenants move in, perhaps what might be compared to a few months' lease. This is to cover any damage brought about by the tenants, or if they should leave without giving due notice. If this is the situation, then the owner can keep part or the majority of the deposit; whatever money is comparable to the damage. If this hasn't been the situation, however, it is the duty of the owner to ensure that the deposit is carefully looked after, so it can be given back to the tenant when they move out.

Security is clearly significant in any home, and much of the time, this is the obligation of an owner if they are leasing a home out. There are numerous guidelines that spread distinctive part of wellbeing. These incorporate principles identifying the safety of gas, electrical and fire.

Under the Gas Safety Regulations 1998, there must be a yearly gas check on all leased homes. All gas apparatuses must be checked to ensure they can be securely used. Gas machines regularly in leased homes include boilers, radiators, gas stoves and gas fires.

Every single electrical machine provided by an owner must be protected before use. Run of the mill electrical devices in a leased home incorporate coolers, coolers, washing machines, broilers and microwaves. If the devices are the property of the tenants, then they are not the owners' responsibility. PAT testing is the ideal approach to guarantee electrical machines are safe to use. These are tests done on devices, for example, those referenced previously. Expert PAT testing organizations can be employed to do these tests.

By law, things like furniture and beds that are part of the tenure must be heatproof. Smoke alarms must be fitted to all homes since 1992. There are no particular rules for homes completed prior to this, yet fire security is part of the 'obligation of consideration,' so landowners could be considered liable for any fire damage, and there are no smoke alarms.

Laws shift from state to state, and it is your responsibility to discover progressively about them. Be that as it may, here are a couple of general rules and questions, which may enable you to find out what your state directs with respect to these issues. Discover basic things like how much time before you can request an increase in the rent, any enthusiasm on the security deposit you have to pay, the longest time you can hold a security deposit after the tenant leaves, any expense you can charge if there should be an occurrence recently installment and to what extent you need to hang on before you can add interest for that expense, and so on.

The tenant contract you draw up is typically dealt with by the lawyer, yet it would not hurt to find out what it contains. Get some answers concerning the different authoritative reports required in your state and how you can tailor these structures/archives to suit your needs. Moreover, become familiar with where these archives get lawfully recorded - related charges, and so on. A decent lawyer can generally see you through the majority of this securely.

It is basic that you think about the lodging demonstrations in your state. Tenants are generally ensured with some basic rights, for example, a home fit for human residence, unlawful separation, capacity to hold the owner at risk if there should be an occurrence of harm caused because of the landowner's carelessness and security against being evited without lawful notice. You have to ensure that you don't waver here, and in the event of conflicts concerning the abovementioned, you do the methodology legally.

With regard to uncovering realities about the rental, you have to cover a scope of issues. A few states may require explicit checks to be done on the house and the outcomes uncovered to the tenants - like sexual stalkers in the area, nearness of radon gas, and so forth. There are both government and state prerequisites in regard to divulging specific facts to tenants, and you should hold fast to these.

The greater part of the above can be dealt with without anyone else's input, yet with removals, you need a decent lawyer and an exhaustive understanding of the laws. If you have a fundamental thought, at that point, don't do anything careless like stopping the power supply in light of late repayment. You have to discover the conditions on which eviction is really appropriate. Moreover, discover the definite strategy, the notice you should serve, the complete expense and so forth. This will enable you to pass judgment if you even need an eviction instead of a settlement out of court. If you do genuinely think about eviction, hire a better than average lawyer.

Appreciating your laws is important as you need to remain well inside the lawful limits. It will make your life less difficult and keep you from settling on careless choices that may cost you dearly.

Landowner tenant laws were made to fill in as an outline for the associations, rights, and commitments of both the owners and tenants. While each state's laws will shift marginally, there are some broad obligations and administrations that each owner must give. Here are five essential commitments each owner must follow, wherever the person in question possesses rental property.

A owner's obligations under landowner tenant law are ordinarily separated into five sections:

1.   Security Deposit

2.   Disclosure of Owner

3.   Delivering Possession of the Unit

4.   Maintenance

5.   Liability

Commitment to Manage Security Deposits or Prepaid Rent

The primary commitment of each landowner has to do with a tenant's security deposit. Each landowner has the privilege to charge their tenants a security deposit even though this deposit never really has a place with the owner. Rather, this deposit is a type of security for the landowner in case the tenant neglects to pay lease, damages the property or generally breaks the rent agreement.

Owners commit to adhere to the statewide and nearby laws concerning the security deposit. For example, certain states set breaking points on the most extreme measure of security a landowner can charge for a deposit. There are additionally explicit principles for putting away the security deposit, restoring the security deposit and how to manage the security deposit if you sell your property. Owners are committed to adhering to these laws, or they can face legitimate ramifications for neglecting to do as such.

Commitment to Disclose Owner

The second commitment each landowner has to uncover to their tenants is certain data about the owner of the property. This obligation lies with the individual who has consented to the rent arrangement with the tenant, regardless of whether it is the structure's owner, the landowner, or another person who is going about as the owner's operator.

What to Disclose

The names and addresses of the individual or people with the ability to deal with the structure, collect rent, make repairs, address objections or issues.

The Most Effective Method to Disclose It

This declaration should be recorded as a hard copy and should happen before the real tenure starts. If any progressions happen during the tenant's occupancy, the tenant must be informed of the change.

Why This Disclosure is Important

The reason for this commitment is to guarantee that the tenant knows the right contact individual for different exercises, for example, lease accumulation and maintenance demands, just as for any other legitimate issues that may emerge.

If this divulgence of the owner isn't made to the tenant, the individual collecting the rent becomes the go-to individual for taking care of all issues identified with the property.

Commitment to Deliver Possession of Unit

The third commitment for owners under the landowner tenant law is to convey ownership of the unit to the tenant. This implies having the unit empty for the tenant, progressing on a date that was indicated in the rent agreement. If the unit isn't accessible for the tenant on the agreed move-in date, the tenant might have the option to seek legitimate activity against the landowner for the inability to respect the rent agreement.

Moreover, if there is a squatter in the unit or another person who doesn't have the lawful right to be there, the owner may seek lawful activity against this person. The owner could be granted damages.

Commitment to Maintain the Unit

An owner has the duty to their tenants to maintain the property. This incorporates keeping the property perfect, sheltered and tenable. The landowner must stick to all construction standards, perform fundamental repairs, keep up normal regions, keep every single indispensable assistance, for example, plumbing, power, and warmth, in great working order, provide appropriate junk repositories and must stockpile running water.

Commitments Subject to Limitation of Liability

A landowner is at risk for following the commitments set out under owner tenant law. This incorporates holding to the provisions of the rent agreement.

In numerous states, a landowner is released of this risk once they sell the property and tell the tenant via a hard copy that the property is under new ownership or management. At that point, the new owner is no longer subject to keeping the provisions of the rent agreement and keeping the landowner tenant law in the state.

CHAPTER SIX
How to Finance Rentals

The mystery in the real estate business is to use other individuals' cash. This is the way most real estate big shots are made. Unlike customary private real estate contracts, real estate financing offers a lot more extensive money-related choices, including loans or financing from different monetary foundations. Exchanges like these call for better than expected arrangement abilities.

It's not prudent to put your own cash into real estate for a couple of significant reasons. To begin with, you will give a large portion of your benefits away by not using your investment. Second, real estate is an extremely dangerous business - you would prefer not to jeopardize all that you have.

It is not necessarily the case that real estate investment is about disasters, despite what might be expected. If you realize how to make cash work for you, you may really accrue a lot of cash as a byproduct of your investment.

Here's the secret:

If you buy a $100,000 property that expands a normal of 7 percent for each year (in reality, that number could be higher or lower), you would see a net benefit from leasing your property, bringing about a roughly 15 percent return.

If you're content with little return of investment, you may settle for your 15 percent return. But if you really need to acquire on your investment, think about what using money can accomplish for you. At present, a common real estate investor can discover financing as high as 95 to 97 percent of the price tag. There are even a few occasions where you might possibly get 100 percent financing, yet we won't use this for our model as it's a deficient correlation.

Along these lines, in case you're an investor who is content with a small return of investment, then 15 percent seems like a great deal. But, for the individuals who really need to become wildly successful in real estate, 15 percent is a long way from being viewed as a vital return.

How does this work?

We expect that the rent payments will cover every one of your costs, including the home loan repayments. Taking a similar model, a 7 percent valuation for your property brings about a $7,000 benefit each year. With 95% financing set up, you'll have the option to get a $7,000 return on $5,000 (your 5 percent initial payment on a $100,000 real estate property). This will furnish you with a 140 percent return on your investment. Moreover, with the equivalent $100,000, you can go out and buy 20 investment properties, money 95% percent of them, and make an astonishing $140,000 benefit a year. This thoroughly beats the $15,000 benefit with an all-money exchange.

Regarding the extra 20 properties, you would experience considerable difficulty in getting financing for them since generally, just five or six new rental property home loans are the most extreme that moneylenders will permit. This is the reason why you need better than expected management abilities.

Innovative Methods for Financing a Rental Property Purchase

The conventional way to purchase an investment property is to set aside cash for an upfront payment, and get a home loan to cover the rest. However, this is not the only way. Every once in a while, I get inquiries from landowners who want to know how they can back a rental property if they need more in the bank for an upfront payment.

Here are four techniques proposed for thought.

1. Dealer Financing

This includes getting an advance from the individual you're purchasing the property from. At times, if the merchant is eager to loan you cash, it's simpler (read: less paperwork) than getting an advance from a bank.

I've seen these arrangements work in various situations. The merchant may back either the initial payment or the full price tag. The merchant may be another property investor — or they may be the property's live-in owner.

The way to progress is to guarantee you agree on a reasonable financing cost for the advance. If you don't have much involvement here, it might be shrewd to work with your CPA or potentially, a lawyer. What's more, paying little heed to how many encounters you have, make certain to get the provisions of the credit recorded as on paper, with marks.

2. Organizations

Another extraordinary financing choice is to collaborate with somebody who has enough cash for an initial payment. This is a compelling system if you have a companion or relative who's keen on engaging in property investment; however, perhaps they'not so fascinated by the everyday work of screening tenants and gathering rent repayments.

In this situation, what frequently happens is that one partner sets up cash, and the other partner handles all the real work of being an owner. The way to progress here is to concede how this would continue. I suggest considering it as far as adjusting the risk and reward to expenses and advantages. Your partner is going out on a limb on all the budgetary risks; however, you're doing all the legwork of acquiring income by means of lease. Ensure the way in which you split continues to mirror your commitments.

Whatever you choose bodes well, it's ideal to have your terms recorded on paper.

3. Government Programs

The Federal Housing Administration (FHA) was established to support homeownership. One of the ways it does that is by offering homebuyers the opportunity to purchase property with only 3.5% down.

While FHA advances are explicitly intended to encourage the sale of owner-involved homes, it's totally reasonable to purchase a two-, three-or four-unit building, live in one unit, and obtain rental pay from the others. Truth be told, this can be an unbelievably savvy approach to back a rental property, particularly if it's your first.

FHA credit cutoff points are distinctive in each region, so part of the skill here is ensuring that as far as possible, where you need to purchase is sufficiently high that you can buy a multiunit property.

4. Retirement Accounts

Many individuals who have moved jobs every now and again or worked for themselves for any time period have retirement cash in an IRA. If you have a self-coordinated IRA, you're permitted to put resources into non-traditional resources, which means an option other than stocks or shared assets. Real estate is an affirmed investment class, which means you can use cash in a self-guided IRA to back a rental property.

If you go this course, however, chat with your CPA first. Indeed, even with programming that makes it simpler to be a landowner, real estate is a bigger number of hands-on investment than anything in the financial exchange. Before you dive in, ensure that you will contribute the time and energy important to see an advantageous degree of profitability.

Keep in mind: Pay Attention to Details

Notwithstanding how you fund your rental property, make sure you have sufficient paperwork set up to set you up for progress and consistent pay from the property you purchase. That implies putting resources into:

• Formal (composed) agreements with a dealer who has consented to loan you cash toward a property buy.

• Legal records like LLC working consent to characterize who does what in an organization (and who gets what remuneration).

• Projections of expected income from different investment types from your monetary organizer, so you can look at potential results.

Putting resources into real estate can be fulfilling and rewarding. To get the best advantage for as long as possible, it's ideal to deal with the details from the earliest starting point.

Financing Multiple Rental Properties

Purchasing various rental properties on the double is a rewarding endeavor, particularly if you are hoping to develop your real estate investment portfolio rapidly. Not exclusively would it be able to enable you to develop your investment portfolio, yet this methodology will also give numerous income streams every month. Things being what they are, doesn't each apprentice real estate investor do this? Since they do not understand how to back various rental properties without a moment's delay. Indeed, the general concept appears to be outlandish for generally amateurs.

Presently, even though it is difficult, we have assembled a couple of alternatives that will enable you to figure out how to fund various rental properties along these lines right away. Here we go!

One Loan, Multiple Rental Units

One approach to back various rental properties is to purchase numerous units in a single structure. A wide range of multi-family real estate fall inside this classification, including condo structures, duplexes and quadruplexes.

So, how can one fund various rental properties of this type?

You can apply for standard home loan credits at the neighborhood bank. It is like the home loan you would get the chance to purchase a house to live in, with a couple of additional necessities, obviously. Be that as it may, you should set something aside for an initial payment for the investment property route before you look for subsidizing. Ordinarily, it is a 20% initial payment. At present, you can discover contract loan specialists who will require less.

Financing Two to Four Rental Properties

How can you back numerous rental properties when you're thinking about purchasing less than five?

You can go to your neighborhood home loan representative or bank for investment property financing. For this number of rental properties, you need the accompanying:

1. A FICO assessment number under 630.

2. An initial payment for investment property prepared.

3. A quarter of a year of money holdings for the ideal home loan payment.

Be that as it may, one thing to remember is the sort of moneylender you go to. It's ideal to maintain a strategic distance from real banks. More often than not, such banks will be careful with their borrowers, so they require stricter criteria. Rather, work with nearby agents and search for banks, which are typically more eager to fund under five rental properties.

Financing Five to Ten Rental Properties

For this number of rental properties, the bank will back your real estate investments if:

1. You have a FICO rating of 720.

2. You have a half year's worth of deposits to guarantee against opportunities.

3. You have an upfront payment of 25% for single-family homes and 30% for multi-family real estate properties.

4. You don't have any history of repossessions or Chapter 11.

5. You didn't fall behind on home loan repayments (for your main living place) for the most recent year.

Financing More Than Ten Rental Properties

For this measure of real estate investment advances, you need to go to significant loan affiliations, for example, the Bank of America. However, much the same as different choices; you should have your financial assessment prepared just like your upfront payment.

Is It Possible to Take Multiple Mortgages for Rental Properties?

Indeed, it is conceivable to take a few home loans on the double to fund numerous rental properties. Nonetheless, the number of home loans will rely on your home loan moneylender and its restrictions. Some will give you a chance to take the same number as is allowed, and others will restrict you, depending on your FICO assessment and capacity to cover payments. Along these lines, for this, you should perform appropriate due persistence.

Step by step instructions to persuade your home loan bank to back different rental properties for you

Most importantly, ensure you are prepared for the amount of paperwork the loan specialist will require. Your home loan moneylender should have the option to compute your obligation to-pay proportion, which changes with each rental property investment you make. Thus, set up the entirety of your budget reports, just like other money-related information that the loan specialist requires. You will require these to affirm your capacity to reimburse the home loan.

Second, incorporate beginning computations of the home loan in your marketable strategy. It must comprise the amount of upfront payment you can give, the sum you anticipate the moneylender should offer and the amount of regularly scheduled payments you can pay. You can use a home loan mini-computer for exact conclusions.

Prior to even talking with a bank about how to back various rental properties, feel free to make sense of certain numbers. Figure all the arrival on investment measurements, for example, the income, the top rate, and the money on money return for every one of the rental properties. You need high rates to persuade them, all things considered. Additionally, examine the area and find out about credit rates just as rental interest in that nearby platform. Finally, set up everything together in a real estate marketing strategy and give it to your home loan banks.

How will you compute all that?

To play out a total and intensive rental property examination, you will require a rental property number cruncher. It will also fill in as a home loan number cruncher by considering how all the home loan information you accommodate influences the ROI of a rental property.

Step by step instructions to Finance Multiple Rental Properties: Other Ways

Despite the number of rental properties you are attempting to subsidize, different techniques may require somewhat more from you. For instance, you can go with a sweeping home loan; however, be prepared to tackle its dangers.

You can also go to hard cash banks. Be that as it may, also, be prepared to repay the home loan in a short period; otherwise, you may be liable for abandonment.

CHAPTER SEVEN
How to Repair and Maintain Properties

Probably the greatest choice you will make as an owner is whether you should enlist a property management organization or not. Numerous landowners oversee properties all alone or with the assistance of a representative, for example, manager. Once in awhile, owners need more help when property issues are confusing. This is when owners need to look for the assistance of real estate property management organizations.

Real estate property management organizations can be a huge resource for your organization, but they don't come cheap. They manage prospects and tenants, sparing you time and stress over advertising your rentals, collecting rent, dealing with support and repair issues, reacting to tenant objections, and also looking after evictions. A decent property management organization brings its skill and experience to your property and gives you the significant serenity that comes with realizing your investment is in great hands.

A real estate management business is a self-employed entity, which means you can stay away from the issues of being a business. Alongside the advantages, enlisting a real estate property management organization is also a costly one. If you are living a long way from your rental property, it will be hard for you to deal with property issues from a far distance. The vast majority of the landowners anticipate finding great tenants to keep up their property in great and appealing condition.

In fact, there are not many landowners who look at their property absolutely as an investment and are not keen on loaning them to any tenants. For this situation, the best choice is to procure a real estate property management to deal with the property and deal with the related issues. Regardless of whether you appreciate hands-on management, you will come up short on time to focus on the development of your business, which means you will need to contract help for your property. Enlisting the help of a real estate property management organization is an appealing choice if you can bear the cost of the expenses. While talking with management organizations, look for statements running somewhere in the range of 5% and 10% of what you gather in rental income.

A rental property will only appreciate long-term tenant maintenance and a satisfactory degree of profitability if it is maintained appropriately. This includes:

- Preventive and continuous maintenance

- Repairs to address issues or breakdowns

- Construction and redesign

The Role and Responsibilities of a Rental Property Manager

Maintains property rentals by promoting and filling openings; arranging and implementing leases; keeping up and verifying premises.

A property manager is an outsider who is contracted to deal with the day by day tasks of a real estate investment. They can deal with a wide range of properties, from single family homes to enormous high rise buildings. The duties can be extensive, including keeping up property rentals by filling openings, arranging and upholding leases, setting and collecting rent, screening forthcoming tenants, taking care of protests, keeping a precise spending plan and maintaining and verifying premises.

The property manager is in the middle of the tenant and you, the owner. They are the "principal line of resistance," and they are there to shelter you and deal with all issues so effectively that furious tenants or specialist organizations are not calling you in the night.

As to physical maintenance and repairs, a portion of their particular duties may include:

• Investigating and settling tenant complaints; reviewing empty units and finishing repairs; arranging remodels; contracting maintenance services; for example, carpentry, plumbing, power, finishing and snow evacuation administrations.

• Supervising repairs.

• Establishing and implementing preparatory strategies and techniques, reacting to crises.

Magnificent property managers are proactive and thorough.

Protection and Ongoing Maintenance

Preventive and progressing support of rental properties requires exhaustive information of the property, its requirements for maintenance, the staffing required to achieve the errands (or contracting with administration experts) and plan to achieve them. The real estate property manager must adjust the expenses of standard and preventive maintenance with the advantages and wanted outcomes. Details on a property supervisor's normal support rundown may include:

• Cleaning of normal regions.

• Landscape upkeep.

• Regular administration to heating and cooling frameworks.

• Periodic examination of plumbing and electrical things.

• Proper maintenance of wood, material and other structural parts.

Repairs and Corrective Actions

Repairs and corrective actions are required when things break or stop working as expected. At times, the repair is of a crisis nature; for example, a heating breakdown in winter, while at different times, these repairs can be booked and done productively in groups. It is the property manager's responsibility to know the distinction and to serve the requirements of the tenants while adjusting costs. It's additionally critical to deal with small issues before they become huge ones.

Development and Remodeling

Development and renovation are part of the office and building support. Redesign or development of the structure may be required:

• For exceptional business prerequisites of a business tenant.

• To correct out of date quality of the structure.

• To oblige uncommon physical needs.

A real estate property supervisor can be extremely gifted at all different elements of management; however, if they fail with regard to office maintenance, the property will encounter a debasement of condition, loss of tenants, and declining rents.

Maintaining a Real Estate Investment Property

What individuals frequently overlook is the significance of dealing with their real estate property. Like anything else in everyday life, your real estate investment property needs uncommon consideration and fastidious consideration to be fruitful and remain effective. So, how can real estate investors maintain their real estate investment property? What is required to keep regular tenants in their rental properties?

Owning a real estate investment property can be exceptionally useful and can turn into a fundamental hotspot for your pay. It accommodates numerous individuals' extraordinary income, leaving them with additional cash, even after all the bills have been paid. The individuals who claim real estate investment properties have the benefit of controlling their prosperity or their disappointment. They get the chance to control the circumstance and their money-related future. Some portion of expanding your prosperity and advantages from your real estate investment property is figuring out how to look after it. There are numerous preferences for keeping your property slick and clean. An all-around maintained property would retain its value and draw in better quality tenants, which advantages the two sides.

Tips and rules on the best way to maintain a real estate investment property:

1. Investigate both the exterior and interior of your rental property

Having your rental property well-kept and free from any damage will build your benefit and enable you to keep great tenants. Unanticipated costs like repairs and replacements are unavoidable when dealing with a rental property, and you shouldn't put them off. Here's what to search for when examining your rental property.

Outdoors

Roof: Verify whether there are missing shingles, damaged blazing or shape and greenery. These can cause expensive damage later on. Additionally, verify whether any tree limbs fall onto your rooftop and cut them off. You need to abstain from having any of these since they can cause real damage.

Windows: Verify whether every one of your windows are fixed appropriately without any holes and if there are holes, seal them. This will spare you later on from dampness and lost heat.

Exterior painting: ensure that the outside of your rental property is constantly painted to shield it from dampness and sun damage. No one needs to live in a house that looks terrible from the outside.

Landscape: Check for broken tree limbs or trees with parasites. Anything that may carry mischief to your tenants, make sure to fix it. Likewise, ensure the grass is sound and consistently cut it so that any new tenant going by can see that your property is well-maintained.

Indoors

Water radiator: Make a point to deplete and consistently remove any soil from the water heaters. If you live in a territory with a great deal of silt in the water, you should seriously think about making this a month to month task.

Smoke detectors: This is certainly an absolute necessity. Continuously ensure that your smoke alarms have new batteries and capacity appropriately. Living in a house with smoke alarms that don't work can be extremely hazardous.

Heating and cooling: Consistently assess the heating and cooling framework. Check the channels and ensure there aren't any plants growing around them. This can limit the wind current and may destroy the framework later on.

Paint: Check for any paint chips or shape that may be on the dividers and consistently re-paint your dividers for a spotless and crisp inside.

2. Keep your tenants happy

Not only should you maintain your real estate investment property by fixing damage, but you should also keep your tenants fulfilled. Only a basic examination to perceive how things are going or inquiring as to whether they need anything will work. Demonstrating to them that you are consistently there to help and that their happiness is your need will really have any kind of effect. This will help your reputation for future tenants and draw in numerous individuals to your rental properties. React to their repair demands. One of the principle reasons tenants move out is because they are upset, so make a point to keep your tenants satisfied.

3. Contract a property director

Dealing with your rental property can turn into a mind-boggling task. It requires some investment and necessitates ordinary checkups. For the individuals who feel it's a lot of burden, they can employ a property director that will maintain their real estate investment property. This is a major choice since these organizations are not cheap, yet consider all the time you will save. A property supervisor can do all that you need from inside to outside to dealing with the month to month lease.

4. Observe the Landlord Occupant Law

Observing the owner tenant law will help you in keeping up your real estate investment property and help you in overseeing it accurately. It will provide structure to both you and the tenant in order to not commit numerous errors and keep your rental property in great condition. One of the commitments under the landowner law is maintenance, so adhering to this law precisely will profit you a great deal.

5. Renovate and Improve

Tenants are continually looking for new and created rentals. As an owner, you ought to consistently consider approaches to refurbish and improve your real estate investment property. For models, including another style of outside plan, such as revamping the yard, including a nursery, or modernizing the inside by including frameless glass dividers. Do some exploration on new interior structures that are moderate. These are great changes that will draw in tenants from everywhere.

Tenants have a right to appreciate protected and tenable living conditions, and it's the homeowner's responsibility to deal with and maintain the property. A well-kept property will help to increase your prosperity and income. Continuously look for ways to settle rental property issues before the issues get greater.

CHAPTER EIGHT

How to Recruit Top Talent to Work on Your Property

As a real estate pioneer or brand, your group is the most valuable resource you have. Having said that, how might you acquire the best real estate talent and keep them?

1. Adaptable work gameplans: Campaign Track suggests offering adaptable work courses of action. This may mean an opportunity in adjusting the available time from home hours. Adaptability can also apply to planning. Given your real estate colleagues deliver the outcomes, does it really make a difference when they do or don't work?

2. Proactively sanction downtime: If your real estate group has adaptability in their calendar doesn't mean they will be compelled to use it. There are a lot of real estate pioneers, CEOs, and investors that could be observing a four hour work week, yet wind up working 100 hour weeks, 52 weeks every year. If you don't proactively help to suit and advance ordinary downtime, you will lose individuals due to burnout. Tragically, as a general rule, it will be your best workers. Think about

inciting and paying them to take a break every year.

3. Limits and advantages: Real estate organizations shouldn't lose everything by offering such a large number of costly advantages; however, they can offer a significant menu of limits. Outsider organizations and specialist organizations will regularly leave a pocket for the limits to enroll the business your real estate organization can offer. This can incorporate protection items, retirement plans and exercise center memberships, autos, lodging, and shutting related administrations. A little can go a long way, according to your representatives.

4. Offers: Real estate business visionaries with a foot in the startup world should now be well aware that giving offers is currently normally expected for key representatives and colleagues. If you are really heading off to some place, offers can be the absolute most alluring and profitable remuneration. Simply ensure you don't damage raising support and development endeavors simultaneously.

5. Training: Helping colleagues improve themselves and develop their capabilities is just going to support your relationship. Ensure you

have a solid program for preparing and developing learning. This can be real estate training or undertaking explicit instruction, just as persuasive and moving occasions.

6. Offer positive outcomes: Don't expect that your colleagues feel valued just because you continue to pay them and haven't terminated them yet. They need to realize that their commitment matters, and that they're doing work that is helping the organization Always spare a moment to tell them.

7. Have the innovation and tools they need: Today, incredible talent is attracted to organizations that can enable them to boost their potential. If you're solid around there, make some noise about it! Maybe you've grown new, game-changing innovation or have put resources into quality devices and structures that your rivals haven't. That ought to be a notable advantage. It could also get others that are similarly able to dispatch their own challenges to turn into a piece of yours.

8. A solid PR campaign: Incredible organizations don't sell themselves. They need PR and proactive online reputation management. Become a magnet for good representatives. What will a Google search or two uncover about you and your group? Is it accurate to say that you are consistently

pushing out positive PR? Will top talent in the real estate industry see you and say to themselves, "I need to figure out how to be a piece of that organization and mission" and proactively search you out?

Workers are not searching for a profession; they're searching for an encounter." They prescribe businesses that center around an encounter that is fulfilling, energizing and enabling.

9. Referrals: One of the ideal approaches to discover top talent in real estate is to use the group and relationships you now have. This expands the chances they'll be a solid match. Have you connected and inquired as to whether they know anybody that would be a decent resource?

Real estate is an exceptionally aggressive industry, perfect for eager and well-informed millennials searching for professional development. The question is, how can you pull in the best talent for your real estate business?

1. Provide adaptability

A focused salary package will consistently be appealing. However, it must be more than the cash for twenty to thirty-year-olds going into real estate and property management. It's not constantly about the dollar for them by any means. In different enterprises, this may prove to be an appealing drawcard, but in property management, they're not battling for more cash; they're battling for adaptability.

Enabling workers to be adaptable in their schedule implies an association values a healthy lifestyle and that their welfare is imperative to their manager. Investigate working from home choices and encourage innovations to streamline business procedures, even outside the workplace.

2. Build a solid and comprehensive hierarchical structure

In enrollment firm, Robert Walters' most recent whitepaper: "Pulling in, holding and creating millennial experts" is one of the main three factors in an organization that is unified with a solid culture. A reasonable and characterized set of hierarchical qualities and culture ought to mirror the millennial's needs of inclusivity, decent variety, and open communication in the work environment. Not only do recent college grads want a strong stimulating culture, but they also want to limit conflict among themselves and older colleagues.

3. Make a bona fide brand

Besides informing prospects regarding the organizational culture and qualities, it's also basic that businesses show it. Advance your organization's culture and present it in a great light. The recruitment supplier, Manpower Group, has recently discovered that Australian job seekers accept that "a business' image and reputation are more significant today than five years ago.

A helpful and best approach to advance a bona fide brand is through an association's current workers by enjoying and sharing organization internet based life presents on their own systems. This should be done naturally because media-sharp millennials appreciate validity above all else.

4. Go social

Apart from using internet-based life channels to advance your image, posting work promotions on social networks as tagged pictures or short videos gives organizations a remarkable chance to draw in and resound with potential representatives.

People somewhere in the range of 18 and 39 years are the most prolific in online network use. Thus, recruitment managers and expert selection representatives believe that the quickest and best approach to enlist Millennials is by concentrating on the social networks of Facebook, Twitter, and LinkedIn.

5. Advance a reasonable methodology for career development

"Twenty to thirty-year-olds need a characterized profession. They need to realize where they will be in 10 years' time," as indicated by Adam Hooley. Let know during the interview that you have a group structure and a lifelong way, and effectively urge new Millennial volunteers to learn and improve their skillset are what will engage this statistic.

Tips for acquiring and holding great property management staff

When you're developing your business, perhaps the greatest test is finding the ideal individuals to advance the organization. Numerous property supervisors are prepared to take their organization to the following level; however, the overwhelming assignment of contracting and holding quality representatives keeps them from making that next step.

We get it—you're fighting patterns of high turnover, low joblessness, and furious challenge to enlist top talent. However, if you're set up to settle on the correct choices while contracting, it's less complex than you might suspect to effectively develop your group.

Here are our four best contracting tips for property management organizations, hoping to pull in and keep the correct individuals to develop your business.

Have a Stand-Out Job Description

A job description is your organization's first introduction to potential applicants, and it's significant that your activity posts are clear, compact, and precisely mirror the position you're recruiting for. A successful set of job responsibilities means that you can eliminate unfit competitors and draw in top talent. Ensure your job description responsibilities check the following boxes:

• Descriptive and quantifiable. Your expected set of responsibilities ought to plainly depict work obligations and obligations, just as quantifiable objectives for what achievement will resemble (for example react to tenant demands inside 24 hours).

• Straightforward necessities. If you've been adopting a reorder strategy to sets of responsibilities, you're likely not contracting effectively. Each new position portrayal ought to indicate the aptitudes and necessities you're searching for—else, you'll be swimming through heaps of unfit candidates with each new position you post.

• Sell your organization. Your job description should address this inquiry for applicants: Why would I want to work here? Offer what's extraordinary about working for your organization, for example, your advantages, work environment culture, and accomplishments. It's alright to boast a little and let applicants know why they ought to bring their talent to your business!

Post on the Top Job Boards

Not all job descriptions are equal. There's such a mind-bending concept as over-posting your employment opportunities, which will result in an excessive number of candidates and insufficient qualified applicants. Be key about where you post and adhere to the most respectable activity sheets:

• Free job descriptions: To share your activity postings for nothing, use sites like LinkedIn, where you'll reach a huge number of applicants right away. Look at nearby, online job sites like network Facebook groups. If you live close to a junior college or college, there's normally an online activity board to communicate postings to undergraduates and staff.

• Sponsored employment sheets: If you're willing to pay a charge, you can support your activity postings on Indeed, Monster, and other major online job sites. Supporting your presence sends your activity to the top of the line, getting it to potential applicants quicker.

Ask the Right Interview Inquiries

You've composed an extraordinary set of responsibilities, you've posted it on the correct sites, and now it's a great opportunity to talk with your up-and-comers. Simple, isn't that so? As a matter of fact, numerous supervisors and owners will tell you that it's similarly as overwhelming (if not more so!) to be on the opposite side of the desk during the interview. If you set up the correct questions ahead of time, you'll end up with the information you need to settle on the correct choice:

• Evaluate work abilities. To become familiar with the applicant's job abilities and encounters, think about posing the following inquiries:

◎ What has been your most prominent accomplishment?

◎ What's an impediment that you've experienced in your work? How did you solve it?

◎ How would your associates at your current job describe you? Shouldn't something be said about your manager?

• Evaluate the employment fit. Employment fit surveys how a competitor's aptitudes, experience, and desires line up with the position you're attempting to fill. To ensure that the applicant is a good fit, ask the following questions:

◎ Why did you leave your latest workplace?

◎ Why do you need this job?

◎ What are your objectives for the future?

• Evaluate the culture fit. At long last, you'll need to comprehend if the applicant fits into your group and your vision for the organization's future. Regardless of whether your business has 3 representatives or 30, you'll need somebody who offers your qualities and your meaning of what achievement looks like. Have a go at asking:

◎ What are the three characteristics that you value most in a co-worker? Shouldn't something be said about a supervisor?

◎ What's the greatest risk you've ever taken, and why?

◎ When working in a group context, which job would you say you are well on the way to take?

Battle High Turnover with Culture and Relationships

When you've contracted the correct applicant, ensure that you have a system set up to retain them. There's a ton of turnover in this industry, and the expense of losing a worker is high. Fortunately, there are a few stages you can do to make a flourishing working environment with faithful employees:

• Provide preparing openings. When workers are offered preparing openings, they realize that the organization has put resources into their development. Send your workers to meetings, put resources into structuring their range of abilities, and make work shadow openings between co-workers.

• Offer modest pay rates and advantages. By the day's end, your workers will possibly stay if you pay them decently and offer benefits that guarantee their success. Keep in mind that there's an expense to losing somebody—it requires some investment and cash to select, contract, and train each new worker.

• Build solid individual connections. Probably, the ideal approach to connect with representatives and build loyalty is to become acquainted with them. Make a situation where you get a lot of exposure with every worker to become familiar with their future objectives and what's essential to them. When an employee cares about their work connections and realizes that you've put resources into their development, they're bound to come to you when there's an issue as opposed to searching for a new position.

CHAPTER NINE

How To Manage a Landlord's Rentals or Find a Property Manager

While these means are spread out in a particular request, it is conceivable that you may need to manage a portion of the means non-consecutively. Depending on the number of properties you manage or your property points of interest, you may wind up chipping away at Step 7 preceding you arrive at Step 3. That is alright!

No guide, regardless of how extensive, can give you a careful play-by-play of what you should do. Rather, use this guide as a general asset to enable you to work through various circumstances as they happen during your time as a property manager.

Stage 1: Buy and Repair

The initial step of dealing with any investment or rental property is to purchase the property and get it into great repair. If you don't have your property yet, or it's not in rentable condition, these are the two things that you have to do from the start.

Numerous elements go into purchasing the correct investment property and fixing it to be profitable.

Because of the number of variables, this guide won't go into those details.

Stage 2: Set Prices and Expectations

When you have control of your rental property and feel that it is ready to be leased, you have one significant thing to finish before you can begin searching for tenants. It's a great opportunity to set up your rental costs and desires.

Statistical surveying in the area

Prior to setting a value, you need to look into the normal rental cost in the region and the number of rental properties accessible. It's possible that you previously did a portion of this exploration during the purchasing procedure.

Make sense of the following:

- What is the normal pay in the area?

- What is the normal family size?

- What is the normal rental cost?

- Does your area have any extra-unique advantages (i.e., public transport, simple parkway access, off-road stopping) that you can charge more for?

As you take in the different rentals available and the going rates, you'll have the option to suitably value your rental property.

List the Tenant Requirements

As well as choosing a month to month lease, you also need to figure out what requirements you have for hoping to move into your property. By having the perfect tenant at the top of the priority list when you start promoting your property, you'll have a superior shot at discovering them.

Think about the following tenant qualities, remembering that it is illegal to harass tenants:

• Minimum pay

• Smoking or no smoking?

• Employment prerequisite

• Minimum credit score

• Past rental history required?

• The number of references required?

Stage 3: Rent Your Property

Presently, this is the most energizing (and troublesome) time of the rental procedure. It's an ideal opportunity to discover new tenants to lease your property to!

Publicizing

You should publicize your property. Promote wherever you can; paying for extra introduction will be justified, despite all the trouble. Try using basic home locales like Zillow as well as area explicit publications, for example, a network magazine.

Discovering Good Tenants

Finding any tenant is not enough; you need to discover great tenants.

Great tenants look after your property, pay their rent on schedule, and don't cause unnecessary issues. It can be a challenge to recognize a decent tenant during the interview procedure; however, this ability will be instrumental.

Use a rental survey to enable you to see whether every potential tenant is a solid match. Keep in mind that you should observe strict principles about what you can and can't get some information about during these meetings. Getting some information about race, handicaps, and family size are essential no-nos. Observing reasonable lodging standards is a prerequisite. To locate a decent tenant, make certain to do the accompanying:

- Confirm their business area and income

- Do a credit and historical verification

- Call their references

- Call their previous landowners

- Have one-on-one, in-person discussions with them

If you don't do these things, you may miss something that shows a terrible tenant. Since screening tenants can be precarious, you may profit by enlisting an outside tenant screening service to enable you to examine all assembled data to locate the best tenants.

Composing and Reviewing Rental Contracts

When you have a top priority, it will be a great opportunity to sign the rental contract. If you've never set up a rental contract, find some good models online to set up your own.

Then again, obtaining a nearby legal advisor to guarantee you don't miss any vital details is a good idea for your initial tenant agreements. From that point, you can take a shot at your own. Make sure to incorporate data about rental repayment timing, eviction strategies, maintenance details, and home principles in the agreement. Moreover, make certain to reveal and collect a security deposit when concluding the understanding.

Survey the Agreement

Before your new tenant signs, go over the rental agreement with them. This will give both of you opportunities to ask questions and explain data in the agreement to make certain that you each have a clear idea of the content of the agreement.

The Walkthrough

Do a final walkthrough, either with the tenant or an outside observer.

Report whatever number of details of the property as could reasonably be expected. These details can be used to counteract any contradictions later over damage, and doing a walkthrough with the customer can avert any future issues.

Stage 4: Check and Maintain

When your tenant has moved into the property, your job will turn out to be increasingly inactive;

however, that doesn't imply that your duties are finished.

As a landowner, you are the tenant's contact point. If they need assistance with the property or have an issue, you ought to be accessible to enable them to resolve the issue quickly and completely.

Rental Visits

There are a couple of advantages to doing rental walkthroughs more than once per year.

To begin with, visiting your tenant at their property and checking in with them that everything is functioning admirably is a phenomenal method to keep the lines of correspondence open. There might be little issues springing up that they hadn't yet answered to you; these walkthroughs are the ideal time to increase some more understanding.

Second, doing a walkthrough will enable you to look at the condition of the property. If your tenant realizes that you will do a bi-yearly walkthrough, they might be more unwilling to do any damage.

Ordinary Maintenance

All properties will require some maintenance. From basic plumbing repairs to light apparatus substitution, you can anticipate that your tenant should call you with issues that may spring up all through their residency in your property.

To enable maintenance to happen all the more quickly, set up the following ahead of time:

• A list of dependable nearby temporary workers

• Contact data for nearby owners who might almost certainly help

• A list of fundamental fix issues that you can fix yourself

• Specific support finance

• Schedule ordinary check-ups of appliances (AC units, water radiators, and so forth.)

Enormous Repairs

While each owner trusts that it won't occur, there is always the likelihood that you should have a major repair while you have your property leased. From a huge burst pipe to a storm causing broad property damage, enormous repairs may occur. If your property needs a critical repair that will require your tenant to move for a brief period, it is your obligation to give them accommodation whenever they have officially paid.

You may also be required to enable them to pay for elective convenience in forthcoming months, depending on the circumstance. In situations where broad damage has been done to the property, you might need to talk with the tenant about finding somewhere else to live and finishing your rent agreement early. It is conceivable to approve this sort of progress.

Stage 5: Collect Rent

As a landowner, one of your most obvious obligations is to collect rent!

Each landowner has an alternate favored strategy for gathering rental repayments. Some still get checks dropped off or sent to them; others use electronic rent collection services that guarantee they get paid quickly and on schedule.

There are advantages and disadvantages to every strategy, and at the end of the day, it's up to you which type you choose. If you do use a web-based technique for rent collection, remember that there will be a charge included, and you should work this expense into your rental cost.

Raising Rent

Because of increasing expenses in the area, you may need to raise the rent. Raising the rent while you have tenants in a property may appear to be inconceivable, yet it might be important to do if there are long-term tenants who intend to remain for a long time.

Reveal the likelihood of a rent increment to your tenants and work with them to check whether they will remain in the property at the new rate or not.

Late Fees

Make certain to expect a late charge for all late rental repayments. If your tenant is routinely late with their rental repayments, make sure that they know about the probability of eviction, should they keep on paying you late.

Occupants will fabricate all reasons in the book for their late repayments, and it's alright to be considerate about their reasons at some stage. In any case, when a tenant starts to consecutively pay their rent late, it's an indication that they may never again have the option to bear the cost of your property.

Implementing an unmistakable strategy about late expenses will guarantee that they don't keep on leasing your property if they can't afford it. Your strategy on late charges should be clarified in the rental agreement. When giving them notice about recent repayment expenses, make sure to incorporate the significant area of the rental contract for their reference.

Stage 6: Evictions

No owner ever needs to wind up in this position; however, it is possible that you could experience an eviction on your property at some point.

New landowners may have no clue what to do in this circumstance, so it is basic that you do some exploration about neighborhood laws to guarantee that you are observing every one of the guidelines.

It is imperative that you record the eviction and experience the whole court process. Regardless of whether you are disappointed with the time that it takes to get a decision and legitimate eviction continuing, you should pull out to the tenant and record the eviction for the courts.

Any attempt to remove the tenant yourself (by changing the locks or some other individual activity) can be viewed as a criminal offense.

Spare yourself the problem and instead, follow these essential advances:

• Give them authority to see, including the extent to which they need to fix the issue that is breaking their rental agreement.

• File the removal with the court if the notice terms are not met.

• Do not acknowledge repayments if you are petitioning for eviction, as it can invalidate the removal procedure.

• Read nearby laws to make certain you don't disrupt any norms.

• Hire an attorney if the laws are confusing for you.

• Wait for the court decision and nearby sheriff to carry out the the actual eviction.

Stage 7: Accounting

Another angle to property management that you may not be comfortable with is the degree of charges and other bookkeeping data that you will deal with.

If you had a property management organization, they would deliver this data in reports for you, yet doing it individually can be increasingly baffling.

To make your business bookkeeping simpler, follow these tips:

1.   Hire a bookkeeper to do your assessments; the expense is justified, despite all the trouble. They'll enable you to expand findings and guarantee a spotless record.

2.   Keep an exhaustive record of all cash spent on support and other fundamental property maintenance; these are deductible.

3.   Set up explicit ledgers for your costs of doing business to guarantee that your own funds don't get mixed up in the business accounts.

4.   Set aside cash to cover charges and different expenses that may astonish you.

It's Time to Be the Best Property Manager

You've chosen to figure out how to manage rental properties for yourself, and that is a remarkable accomplishment! Since you know the fundamentals of property management, the best way to end up experienced at each progression is to place this learning energetically.

Keep in mind that in its most moderate structure, property management requires just a couple of basic advances:

• Buy and fix a property

• Set up rental expense and tenant prerequisites

• Find tenants and lease the house to them

• Maintain the property

• Collect rent and cover government expenses

• Profit

Try not to progress toward becoming overwhelmed at the idea of dealing with your properties. Being a owner is rewarding work, and you can help to improve your own riches by remaining organized and alert through the procedure. You can be an extraordinary owner; you should simply attempt it!

Top Secrets to Finding the Best Property Manager

Possibly you want to deal with the property yourself? Maybe.

If you use my tips to locate a remarkable management organization, they'll get you more cash than the fee you're paying them.

Consider that. You'll do less work; however, set aside more cash.

The ideal rental property management organization acquires their management charge, and that's only the tip of the iceberg. They can improve your results if you were doing this on your own.

They have more involvement:

- Finding tenants

- Dealing with killjoy tenants

- Collecting late rent

- Doing removals

- Finding reasonable costs and getting limits from contractual workers

- Knowing what repairs are essential (and superfluous) for rentals

- Knowing which areas are best for rentals

- Pricing rentals

- And a whole lot more...

To emphasize, these organizations wind up being worth definitely more than their fees simply through their contacts, expertise, and understanding of the rental market.

Once more, this is possibly valid if you locate a suitable management organization. There are also a lot of terrible organizations that will cost you more cash and be useless at it.

This is where following these tips come in! There are a lot of books and blog entries about managing rental properties yourself.

What a cerebral pain! You are paying a property management organization for specialization and expertise that you can get from reading books and online journals yourself. This will sound 'sales repy;' however, it's valid. It is working incredibly well for me, and it can work for you. I have twenty single-family homes, and they are generally being managed by a similar rental property management organization. I've built up a framework and fabricated a group over recent years that is really working for me (truly and metaphorically).

The most significant piece of this framework is the rental property management group.

Here are privileged insights for finding the ideal one.

1. Read the fine print

When you acquire a rental property management organization, they make you sign an agreement. You need to examine this agreement cautiously. There is something explicit I need you to look out for.

Ensure they don't make it difficult to fire them.

The agreement will have something in it that decides under what conditions you can end the rental property management contract with them.

If you end the agreement, you might need to pay a couple of more months of their management expenses. It might even say you need to pay the remainder of the year. Understand this language. If you feel they are performing seriously and need to quit using them, ensure that you see the amount it will cost you to leave. You also need to understand how you can legitimately drop the agreement. You may need to accomplish something recorded on paper or by registered mail.

I had this part of the agreement removed from my contract. If I was discontent with the management organization's administration, I had the option to end without paying any extra-long stretches of management charges.

Ensure you have the alternative to dispose of the property management organization if important, and ensure it doesn't cost you to an extreme.

2. Check their expenses

Start by looking at their management contract and understanding their expense structure.

The most essential charge to understand is how they would charge management. Normally, it is a level of lease. 10% of the lease is normal; however, I've seen numerous places charge less. 8% isn't unprecedented.

It's much the same as some other expense structure throughout everyday life. When an organization charges 8% rather than 10%, you might see that in some other part of the expense structure, they might be more costly than a contender. They will find somewhere else to compensate for it.

A genuine case of this is shown with my present rental property management organization. They charge 10%, which some may state is high, yet they don't charge an expense for discovering tenants and marking a rent. They additionally don't charge an expense for leaving a rent once it lapses. A great deal of other property management organizations do.

Numerous organizations charge a month's lease or possibly a large portion of a month's lease for marking a rent. This can be significant in ascertaining your costs.

My turnover rates in Montgomery, Alabama are very high. The normal turnover is between 1½ to 2 years. It would cost me a fortune to pay a month's rent each time that occurs, so having this incorporated into my 10% expense is brilliant.

If you were in an area where turnover was lower, possibly an expense of one month's rent wouldn't be good enough for you. A few people lease a similar house for five or ten years. See how your management organization will charge you for using outside temporary workers. They may charge you the expense of the contractual worker in addition to a rate markup. They may also have their very own contractual workers that they have their own expense framework with. Ensure you get it and contrast it with other management organizations in the region.

The eviction procedure is diverse state-to-state, so the time it takes and the amount it costs can fluctuate enormously. The expense of court and charges that should be paid additionally differ. Ask them to clarify the eviction procedure to you. You have to see how long it usually takes and most dire outcome imaginable. You additionally need to see the amount it will cost you in the two cases to get somebody out of the house. Ask how regularly it occurs and what their screening procedure is to attempt to keep away from it.

3. Would you be able to confide in them?

The primary place to look is checking with online sources.

Check the better business authority. You'll have the option to check whether they are enrolled and if there are any protests against them and how these complaints were settled.

Next, do loads of research online. Check for surveys on them or potential grievances about them. Be careful with an organization that appears to have no online presence of any sort. That is a warning sign. Either they are excessively new, or they're concealing something. You have to check the better business authority, Google their organization name, and use any other online asset you can consider to identify what individuals are stating about them.

Next, request references. Tell them that you might want authorization to talk with different investors who use their management services. In a perfect world, you should talk with at least three. Address a portion of their leaseholders too. See how they are treated by the management organization. These are references that the property management organization give you, and these will have limited usefulness. There is an inclination. They realize you are calling and why, and they feel obliged to express pleasant words. They may even be "friends" of the management organization or investors or leaseholders that show signs of improvement than different clients.

Why does that make a difference?

Because you need an example of how the normal investor or tenant is being dealt with.

In a perfect world, you will figure out how to build up your very own references. You do this by asking the reference that you were given if they know any other person you can talk to. This might be somebody who will give an increasingly legitimate or unprejudiced supposition.

The references you create yourself are more powerful than the ones given to you from the organization.

If the organization is hesitant to give references, this is known as a piece of information. You might need to reexamine. Likewise, if the management organization doesn't work with any investors, this may also be of concern. You'll be the first. That doesn't mean it's a no-go, but it implies that they don't have much understanding, and you won't have the advantage of addressing different investors who can vouch for previously being satisfied with their administration.

How amenable would they say they are? How expert would they say they are with your request? These are what I decide from these telephone calls.

A major issue would be never finding solutions by email and not breaking through to an individual by telephone. Another would be inconsiderate or amateurish responses to questions. I would also be concerned if they appeared to be fine with leasing to individuals with really awful credit or no pay. When I've fulfilled that test, I proceed to talking with the owners of the property management organization.

4. Meet the owners and workers

You need to do this face to face. Specifically evaluating their dependability is something you can't put a cost on. If you are doing this from a far distance, at that point, Skype or video is your final hope, although you could fly or drive out and get this going face to face. Try not to do it by telephone; you need the option to look at one another without flinching and become more acquainted with them on an individual level.

It's a great opportunity to play twenty questions. I'm not restricting you to twenty, this is only the name of that game you sometimes play in the car on long trips. Set up an extensive list of questions that you need to ask about how they deal with each possible circumstance you can consider–everything that worries you as a landowner. How will they handle it for you? Pets, awful credit, late charges, somebody who trashes the house, somebody who won't move out, claims, atomic war, what occurs if this organization fails, anything you can consider.

Here's a list of questions you can start with:

- How old is your organization?

- How did you begin managing real estate?

- How much experience do every one of you have in the real estate business? Property management business? Give me details.

- How many rental properties do you claim yourselves?

- How many rental properties do you manage for investors?

- How wide a range of real estate investors would you say you are managing?

- Will you permit me to address a portion of these investors about their experience working with you?

- How do removals work in this state and city? How long does it usually take and the most pessimistic scenario? How would you handle evictions, and how will I be normally charged for it and the most pessimistic scenario?

- What are your opportunity rates?

• Do you have your own contractual workers that work for you solely? How many do you have and how would you charge me to use them?

• What is your criteria and pay prerequisites for screening tenants?

• What is your pet arrangement?

• Can I see an example rental report that you send investors every month?

• Will you permit me to address a portion of your tenants about their experience working with you?

• Do you have an alternative arrangement for my properties if you choose to quit managing rentals?

You need to anticipate genuine answers should be given for every one of these inquiries. If there is hesitance or hesitance to reply, that's not a decent sign. As I would like to think, you don't need a management organization that is pristine and doesn't have any understanding. You also don't need a management organization that is so enormous, they are not willing to meet with you and answer these questions. If you are simply one more number to them, you'll presumably get poor administration. They ought to be eager to meet with you and answer questions like this to get your business as an investor.

Now, ideally you have enough data about the property management organization to realize you could contract them. There is another significant advance that is just conceivable once they are enlisted and effectively managing it for you. It is guaranteeing them superb administration.

5. Guarantee you are getting quality administration

You have done all your homework and contracted what you accept to be a quality organization. The work doesn't end there. You are going to discover they do things that you don't care for. This might be their strategic approach, awful choices, bookkeeping issues, slow in taking care of opportunities, or any number of issues.

Interestingly, you plainly convey what you are unhappy with, and get them to fix that conduct. Keep in mind, you are paying them a charge for a service, and you anticipate certain things for that expense. Basically, you are preparing them to be the ideal property managers.

In working with our management organization, once in awhile, we find that it is uncertain how cash was spent from the monthly budget report. We quickly talk with the owners and explain why there is confusion over where cash went a month ago. This consistently brings about an increasingly improved monetary report the next month. This makes recording charges and understanding our benefits and misfortunes a lot simpler.

Another genuine model is the treatment of opening. If you see that it is taking the management organization longer than it ought to fill an opportunity, call them and get some information about it. Check how they have it publicized. Get some information about the cost and whether you should possibly offer a move in exceptional or some sort of motivating force to get it leased.

This should bring about improved dealing with openings as time goes on. If it doesn't, then you must have increasingly genuine discussions with them. Opening can be an intense issue for you, particularly if you have a home loan to pay.

Do you recollect my model, where I terminated a management organization because they quoted me a few thousand dollars to fix the stairs, and when I send a jack of all trades over, he fixed it for $50? I would prescribe planning something now and again just to keep everyone genuine.

If there is some kind of enormous offered going on, get a couple of statements from the management organization. You would then tell the management organization that you are also sending over a temporary worker that a friend recommended to get an offer too. You'll only need to do this every once in awhile as a method for ensuring that their offers are reasonable. It's classified "trust, yet check." Trust however check, basically implies I don't confide in you yet, so I need to confirm. There is nothing amiss with that. Individuals that look and appear to be straightforward do obscure stuff and frustrate us now and then. Remember to trust, however, confirm. I think that it's a terrible sign if you get burnt by your management organization along these lines. A cheat is a cheat. You need to fire them.

A few people will choose to manage properties themselves. As I referenced before, an exceptional property management organization has so much experience and contacts that they more than compensate for the charges you pay them. You profit over the long-term by using that learning and experience.

By following my tips, you will get rid of the rotten ones and discover extraordinary management organizations that will progress toward becoming great partners in your real estate business. You will profit for them, and they will produce important automated revenue for you.

It will be a genuine and success win in the organization.